Macmillan
ENCYCLOPEDIA
OF SCIENCE

12

Tools and Tomorrow

Robin Kerrod

Macmillan Publishing Company
New York

Maxwell Macmillan International Publishing Group
New York   Oxford   Singapore   Sydney

Published by:
Macmillan Publishing Company
A Division of Macmillan, Inc.
866 Third Avenue, New York, NY 10022

Collier Macmillan Canada, Inc.
1200 Eglinton Avenue East, Suite 200
Don Mills, Ontario M3C 3N1

Planned and produced by Andromeda Oxford Ltd.

Copyright © 1991 Andromeda Oxford Ltd.
Macmillan edition copyright © 1991 Macmillan Publishing Company

Library of Congress Cataloging-in-Publication Data

Macmillan encyclopedia of science.
    p.   cm.
   Includes bibliographical references and index.
   Summary: An encyclopedia of science and technology, covering
such areas as the Earth, the ocean, plants and animals, medicine,
agriculture, manufacturing, and transportation.
   ISBN 0-02-941346-X (set)
   1. Science–Encyclopedias, Juvenile. 2. Engineering–
Encyclopedias, Juvenile. 3. Technology–Encyclopedias, Juvenile.
[1. Science–Encyclopedias. 2. Technology–Encyclopedias.]
I. Macmillan Publishing Company   90-19940
Q121.M27 1991   CIP
503 – dc20   AC

Volumes of the *Macmillan Encyclopedia of Science*
 1 *Matter and Energy* ISBN 0-02-941141-6
 2 *The Heavens* ISBN 0-02-941142-4
 3 *The Earth* ISBN 0-02-941143-2
 4 *Life on Earth* ISBN 0-02-941144-0
 5 *Plants and Animals* ISBN 0-02-941145-9
 6 *Body and Health* ISBN 0-02-941146-7
 7 *The Environment* ISBN 0-02-941147-5
 8 *Industry* ISBN 0-02-941341-9
 9 *Fuel and Power* ISBN 0-02-941342-7
10 *Transportation* ISBN 0-02-941343-5
11 *Communication* ISBN 0-02-941344-3
12 *Tools and Tomorrow* ISBN 0-02-941345-1

Printed in the United States of America

Introduction

The word "science" comes from a Latin word meaning "to know." In their efforts to know and to understand, scientists must carefully observe, measure, and analyze. This volume examines the instruments and techniques they use, and then looks at the challenges they face now and in the future, on Earth and in space. A special section contains brief biographies of many important scientists and inventors in history.

To learn about a specific topic, start by consulting the Index. It lists page references for the subjects covered in the encyclopedia.

If you come across an unfamiliar word while using this book, the Glossary may be of help. A list of key abbreviations can be found on page 87. If you want to learn more about the topics in the book, turn to the Further Reading section.

Scientists tend to express measurements in units belonging to the "International System," which incorporates metric units. This encyclopedia accordingly uses metric units (with American equivalents also given in the main text). For detailed information on units of measurement, and on numbers, see pages 86-87.

Contents

Part One

Tools of the trade

Throughout history we human beings have used our ingenuity to improve our capabilities and give us greater control over the world in which we live. We have developed tools and machines, and harnessed different forms of energy to extend our limited muscle power. And we have devised many kinds of instruments and devices to extend our imperfect senses. They enable us to see things invisible to the eye, such as minute viruses; and hear things inaudible to the ear, such as ultrasonic waves. They can also detect things that we cannot sense at all, such as gamma rays and X-rays.

This part of the encyclopedia looks at a selection of the instruments scientists and engineers use to measure, view, analyze, and probe. They vary from the kind of weighing scales used in ancient Egypt to huge modern atom smashers, or particle accelerators.

◄ An artificially colored image from a bubble chamber. This instrument helps us observe particles even smaller than atoms, called subatomic particles, which are produced in particle accelerators.

Measuring

Spot facts

- The basic unit of length in the International System of Units, the meter, is defined as the distance traveled by light in 1/299,792,458 of a second.

- The second is defined as 9,192,631,770 cycles of certain radiation emitted by atoms of the cesium-133 isotope.

- The basic International System unit of mass, the kilogram, is the mass of a small cylinder made of platinum-iridium alloy. Called the international prototype kilogram, it was made in 1889 and is preserved at the International Bureau of Weights and Measures at Sèvres, near Paris.

- The lengths of the sides of the square base of the Great Pyramid of Khufu (Cheops), completed about 2580 BC, vary by less than 15 cm (6 in.) from the mean length of 230.36 m (755.8 ft.)

▶ Weighing mussels (moules) in a shop in L'Aiguillon-sur-Mer, on the west coast of France. The woman has scooped up mussels in a measuring container and is pouring them into a bag to be weighed before sale.

Measuring is as old as civilization. It became necessary as societies became more organized. Times and dates had to be fixed for religious and civic ceremonies, goods had to be weighed in trading, and dimensions had to be marked out in building construction. Without accurate measurements, our modern technological civilization of ingenious structures, machines, instruments, and devices could not exist. Scientists could not carry out their work in such depth or get accurate values for their results. Science and technology would founder.

Standards

Some 5,000 years ago, the ancient Egyptians had various weights and measures. For example, they used different-sized stones for weights, and measured lengths in a unit called the cubit. This was the distance from a person's elbow to the tip of the middle finger. But everybody's cubit was different. So a "royal cubit" (52.4 cm, or 20.6 in.) was established as a standard.

The Romans adopted a different cubit, dividing it into 2 feet, and each foot into 12 *unciae* (inches.) For distance measurement they used *mille passus* – one thousand paces. On this, the mile, which is slightly longer, was based. The Romans also established a standard pound (*libra*) for weight. The abbreviation for pound (lb) is based on the Latin word.

The relationships between divisions of the standard weight, length, and so on, were arbitrary. In the U.S. customary system, for example, there are 12 inches in a foot, 3 feet in a yard, 22 yards in a chain, and so on.

It was to simplify matters and establish new standards that a commission of French scientists in the 1790s developed the metric system. It was based on a length unit called the meter: one ten-millionth of the distance between the poles and the Equator, measured along a meridian. The meter is about 3.28084 feet. Larger and smaller units were derived from it as multiples or subdivisions of 10. Other basic units were established: for example, gram for weight and liter for capacity, with derived units again as multiples or subdivisions of 10. (The gram is about 0.035274 ounce, and the liter 1.05669 quarts). In 1960 scientists adopted the system based on the meter, kilogram, and second: the International System of Units (SI).

▼ Early means of measurement. Ancient devices like the water clock (clepsydra) were accurate enough for their age. But precision instruments such as the micrometer and sextant became necessary as technology progressed.

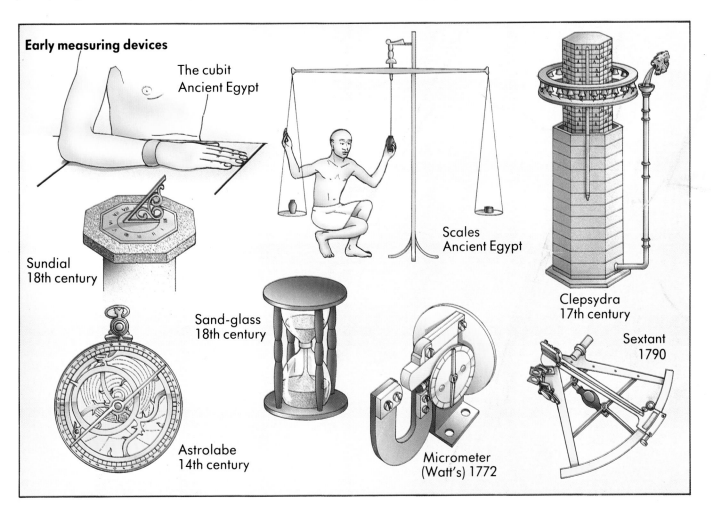

Early measuring devices

The cubit
Ancient Egypt

Sundial
18th century

Scales
Ancient Egypt

Clepsydra
17th century

Sand-glass
18th century

Sextant
1790

Astrolabe
14th century

Micrometer
(Watt's) 1772

Weight

Scales to measure weight were first introduced by the ancient Egyptians before 3500 BC to weigh gold. Illustrations in the famous papyrus known as the *Book of the Dead* show what these scales were like. They consisted of two pans hung from the ends of an arm suspended in the middle. The object to be weighed was placed in one pan, and weights were added to the other pan until the object and weights balanced each other and the arm was again level.

Scales like this are still in use today in markets and stores in many parts of the world. They are what we call equal-arm balances. The same principle is also used in the traditional precision balances once used in every chemical laboratory. In these, the balance arm pivots on a sharp knife edge made of agate or similar material. The pans also hang from knife edges. A pointer attached at right-angles to the arm indicates on a scale when the arm is in balance.

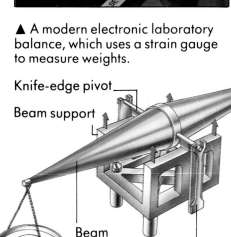

▲ A modern electronic laboratory balance, which uses a strain gauge to measure weights.

▼ This chemical balance was made by Jesse Ramsden in England in 1787. It can measure to the nearest one-thousandth of a gram. (1g is less than ¹⁄₂₈ oz.) The cone-shaped beam pivots on a steel knife-edge when the beam support is raised. Knife-edge pivots were used before electronic ones came into use.

▲ Strain gauges are not only used in balances to measure light weights in the laboratory. They are used to measure heavy weights as well, from elephants to 350-metric ton jumbo jets. Aircraft are weighed every few years to check for changes in weight from paint, dust, and modifications to on-board equipment.

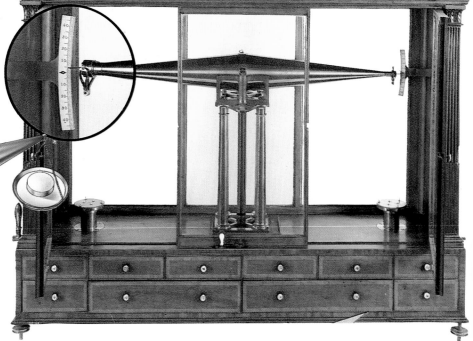

Knife-edge pivot

Beam support

Beam

Y-shaped rests

Weighing pan

Also common are single-pan balances, in which the pan and a cradle of weights are balanced by a counterweight. The object to be weighed is placed in the pan, and weights are removed from the cradle until the arm is in balance again.

Such balances, enclosed in a glass case to prevent disturbance by air currents, can weigh to an accuracy of up to one-thousandth of a gram (1g is less than 1/28 oz.) Much more accurate are the so-called microbalances, which can measure with an accuracy of up to one-millionth of a gram. Some, called torsion balances, employ the twisting action of quartz fibers to restore balance. Others use the electro-magnetism set up by passing electric current through a coil as the restoring force.

The latest laboratory balances are electronic, and are often based on a strain gauge. This is a ribbon, usually of metal, which is stretched by the applied load. Stretching slightly changes the ribbon's electrical resistance. The changes are detected by microcircuits and can be interpreted as weights.

Other everyday balances work on different principles. Spring balances measure weight by the stretching of a spring under load. There may be a rack-and-pinion system that moves the pointer over a scale. The load on some simple scales is balanced by a weighted pointer.

Spring balance

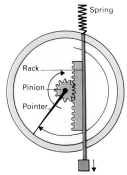

▲ ▶ A spring balance being used at a salmon fishery in Scotland to weigh the day's catch. The balance measures weight as the increase in length of a spring. A toothed rack attached to the spring turns a toothed pinion as it is pulled downward. And a pointer attached to the pinion moves over a scale.

Balance with weighted pointer

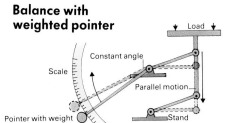

▲ In this balance no spring is involved. If an object is placed on the load pan, it causes a weighted arm to move upward to restore balance. This causes an attached pointer to move over a scale.

Length and distance

Measuring sticks, or rulers, for measuring length date back 5,000 years or more. And, along with flexible measuring tapes, they are still in widespread use in everyday life.

In industry the need for more accurate measuring devices than rulers became pressing as the Industrial Revolution got under way in the late 1700s. Machines just had to fit together accurately. To make accurate measurements, engineers like James Watt, the Scottish steam-engine manufacturer, built micrometer calipers. These relied on the movement of a spindle driven by the rotation of a screw along a screw thread. This gave an accuracy of fractions of a millimeter (1 mm is about $\frac{1}{25}$ in.).

Later, using precision screw-threaded machines, Joseph Whitworth in England produced sets of gauges of standard dimensions for

Triangulation

The classical method of surveying land to make maps, called triangulation, makes use of the geometry of the triangle. The surveyor first measures out a baseline. Then from each end he or she measures with a theodolite (picture) the angle between the baseline and a distant point. From these measurements the distances to the point from each end of the baseline can be simply calculated.

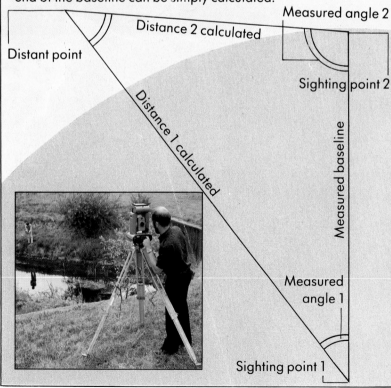

Distant point

Distance 2 calculated

Measured angle 2

Sighting point 2

Distance 1 calculated

Measured baseline

Measured angle 1

Sighting point 1

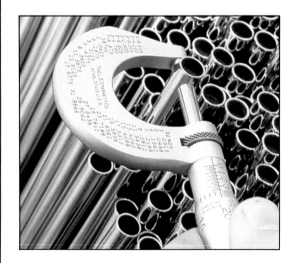

▲ A micrometer caliper being used to measure accurately the external diameter of steel tubing. Rotating the thimble (handle) of the micrometer drives forward a spindle until it touches the tubing. The diameter is then read from fixed and moving scales.

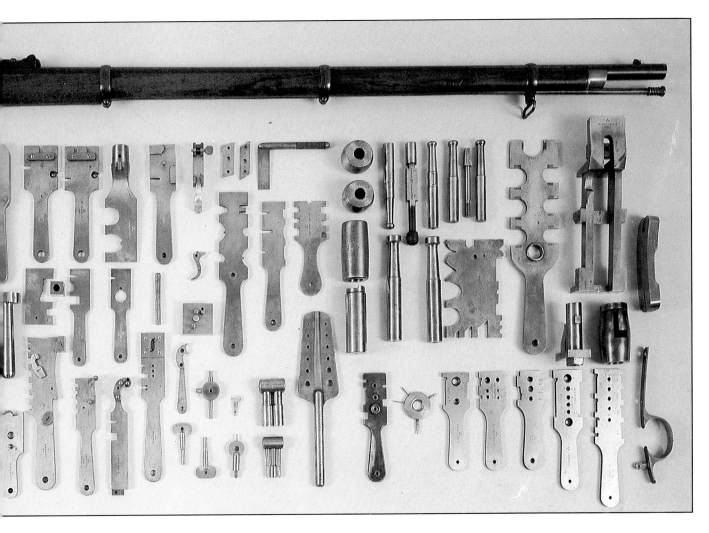

▲ The mass-produced Royal Enfield rifle used by British infantry from the mid-1850s. It was assembled from standardized parts made using this set of accurately measured "slip" and "go-no-go" gauges.

engineering use. Armed with a suitable set of gauges, workers could produce nearly identical, or interchangeable, parts. The assembly of such parts made mass production possible.

For measuring distance, surveyors traditionally use a long steel tape. In earlier times a measuring chain, made up of standard-sized links, was widely used. In recent years surveyors have begun using electronic distance measurement (EDM). Beams of infrared light, for example, are reflected off a target object. The time interval between transmission and reception of the reflection provides a measure of the distance. Range finders working on the same principle and using laser beams are now

widely used by the military.

The vast distances to the stars present a greater problem. Distances to some of the nearest ones are measured by exploiting parallax, the apparent shift in position of an object against a more distant background when it is viewed from two different positions. The distance of far-off galaxies can be gauged from the spectrum of their light. Astronomers know that the more distant a galaxy is, the faster it is traveling away from us. This causes a shift in dark lines in its spectrum towards the red end. From the amount of red shift, the distance to the galaxy can be estimated.

To express astronomical distances, ordinary units of length are inadequate. And astronomers often express distances in terms of the distance light travels in a year (over 9 trillion km, or nearly 6 trillion mi.), calling this a light-year.

Time

Unlike the meter and the kilogram, the SI unit of time, the second, does not fit into a decimal (10-based) system. Sixty seconds make one minute; 60 minutes make one hour; and 24 hours make one day. This way of dividing the day goes back to Babylonian astronomers more than 5,000 years ago. They selected these divisions because their number system was based on 60.

The early peoples told the time by day from the position of the Sun in the sky, and by night from the position of the stars. They devised shadow clocks and sundials to indicate the passage of time by day, and water clocks to tell the time by night.

Not until the 1300s did more accurate mechanical clocks appear in Europe. The first ones used a swinging arm called a foliot as a regulator, a device that repeats its action in a standard time. On each swing, the foliot let escape one tooth of a gearwheel (escape wheel) to move the clock hand. Later clocks used a pendulum as a regulator.

The early clocks were driven by falling weights. They became portable, as watches, after spiral springs (mainsprings) were used instead in the fifteenth century. The watch was later improved by the introduction of a hairspring as regulator. In the modern mechanical watch, this is linked with a balance wheel.

In the modern world mechanical clocks and watches have been largely overtaken by electronic ones, which use a quartz crystal as regulator. Precision quartz-controlled clocks are used for accurate time measurements in scientific work, but they are calibrated against atomic clocks. These clocks are regulated by the frequency of radiation from atoms, often cesium atoms. The standard atomic clock varies by only one second in 1,000 years.

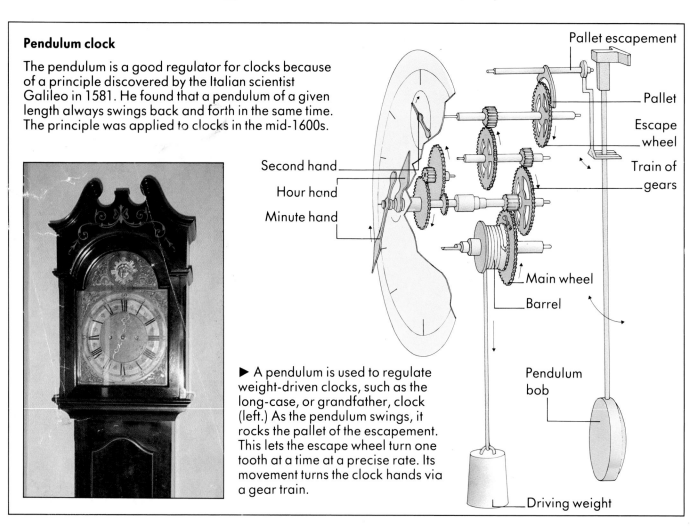

Pendulum clock

The pendulum is a good regulator for clocks because of a principle discovered by the Italian scientist Galileo in 1581. He found that a pendulum of a given length always swings back and forth in the same time. The principle was applied to clocks in the mid-1600s.

Pallet escapement

Pallet

Escape wheel

Train of gears

Second hand

Hour hand

Minute hand

Main wheel

Barrel

Pendulum bob

Driving weight

▶ A pendulum is used to regulate weight-driven clocks, such as the long-case, or grandfather, clock (left.) As the pendulum swings, it rocks the pallet of the escapement. This lets the escape wheel turn one tooth at a time at a precise rate. Its movement turns the clock hands via a gear train.

Digital watch

Quartz crystal is a piezoelectric material. This means that if it is deformed, it produces a tiny electric current. The reverse is also true: if an electric current is applied to it, it will deform. A quartz crystal is used as the regulator in digital watches. When a tiny electric current from a battery is applied to it, it is made to vibrate at a precise frequency of 32,768 hertz (cycles per second). Electronic circuits on a chip reduce the frequency in stages to one vibration per second, and this is then used to drive a digital display that shows the time. Most watches these days have a liquid crystal display (LCD). Early ones used light-emitting diodes (LEDs).

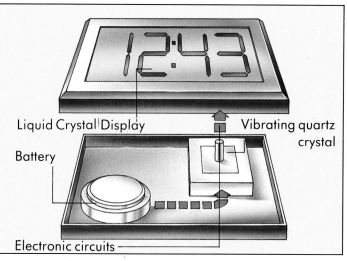

Liquid Crystal Display

Vibrating quartz crystal

Battery

Electronic circuits

Cesium atomic clock

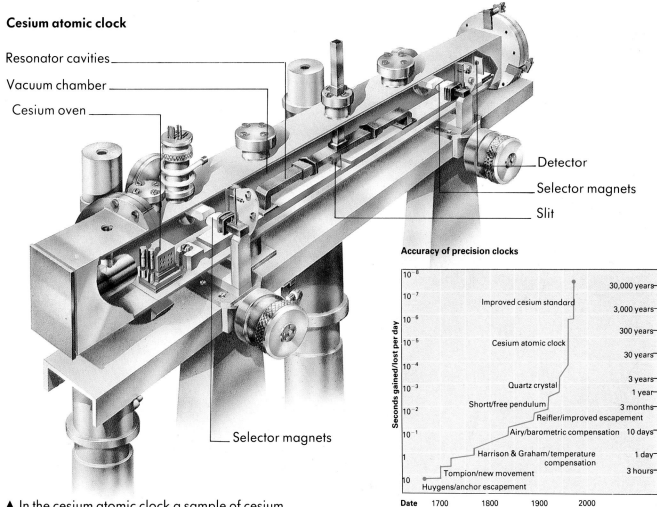

Resonator cavities

Vacuum chamber

Cesium oven

Detector

Selector magnets

Slit

Selector magnets

Accuracy of precision clocks

▲ In the cesium atomic clock a sample of cesium metal is heated and emits atoms, which travel down the tube. Halfway along they pass through a cavity fed with microwaves vibrating at a frequency set by a quartz clock. When this frequency matches the frequency of the cesium atoms, which is 9,192,631,770 hertz, the detector registers maximum.

▲ The accuracy of clocks has improved with each new development. Atomic clocks have brought about the most dramatic improvement. U.S. scientists are now developing one that should be accurate to one second every 10 billion years.

Electricity

Scientists and engineers use a wide variety of electrical instruments for measuring, and for displaying and recording experimental data. In essence most electrical instruments measure either current (rate of flow of electricity) or voltage (electrical "pressure difference").

An ammeter ("amp-meter") measures current in units named amperes (amps), after the French physicist André-Marie Ampère. The standard instrument is a moving-coil meter. The current to be measured is fed through a wire coil located within the poles of a permanent magnet. The passage of the current sets up in the coil a magnetic field. This interacts with the permanent field, and the coil is forced to turn. Attached to the coil is a pointer, restrained by a spring, which indicates the level of current on a marked scale.

A voltmeter is a similar instrument used to

▼ The diagram shows the essential features of a moving-coil meter. The photographs show two views of a type widely used in industry, which can be set to measure electric current, voltage, and resistance.

Liquid crystal display (LCD)

Liquid crystals twist light passing through them. In an LCD that shows blank (left), light passes through a polarizing sheet, which lets through light vibrating in one plane only. It passes through the liquid crystal and then through another polarizing sheet before being reflected back by a mirror. But when current is applied (right), the crystal no longer twists the light. And no light is reflected, because it cannot reach the mirror. As a result, the display shows black.

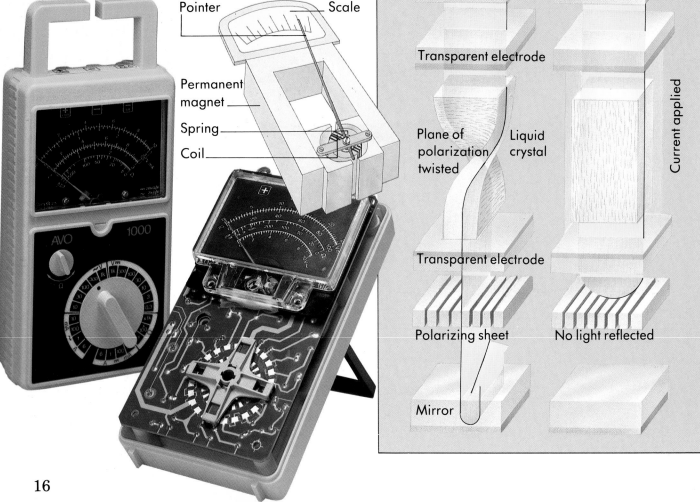

Pointer — Scale

Permanent magnet

Spring

Coil

Blank — Black display

Polarizing sheet

Transparent electrode

Plane of polarization twisted — Liquid crystal

Transparent electrode

Polarizing sheet — No light reflected

Mirror

Current applied

measure voltage in volts, units named after the Italian inventor of the electric battery, Allesandro Volta. It measures the current flowing through a resistor of known electrical resistance, and this is directly related to the applied voltage.

In this type of voltmeter, however, some current is lost in the meter itself. To avoid this inaccuracy, a potentiometer is used. This is a device which balances the unknown voltage against a standard voltage source by means of a sliding resistance. When the voltages are equal, no current flows through the circuit meter, and so no inaccuracy is introduced.

Ammeters and voltmeters can also be used indirectly to measure nonelectrical quantities, such as pressure, rates of flow and temperature. They can do so if these quantities can be suitably converted, or transduced, into electric current and voltage. For example, temperature can be measured electrically with a resistance thermometer. This often uses a coil of platinum wire as a transducer. The resistance of platinum alters as the temperature alters, so current passed through the wire will vary according to the temperature and be a measure of that temperature.

Electrical measurements can also be displayed, notably on an oscilloscope. This is a cathode-ray tube, like the tube in a television set. In the tube a cathode emits a stream of electrons which are focused in a narrow beam onto a fluorescent screen. When electrical voltage is applied to magnetic coils around the tube, the beam is deflected up and down. Usually it is also swept from side to side across the screen, and this gives a visual image of how the applied voltage is varying.

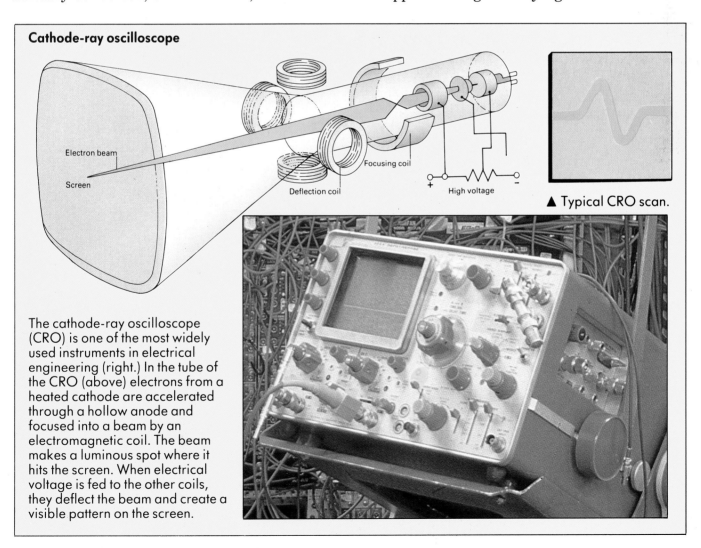

Cathode-ray oscilloscope

Electron beam

Screen

Deflection coil

Focusing coil

+ High voltage −

▲ Typical CRO scan.

The cathode-ray oscilloscope (CRO) is one of the most widely used instruments in electrical engineering (right.) In the tube of the CRO (above) electrons from a heated cathode are accelerated through a hollow anode and focused into a beam by an electromagnetic coil. The beam makes a luminous spot where it hits the screen. When electrical voltage is fed to the other coils, they deflect the beam and create a visible pattern on the screen.

Seeing near

Spot facts

• Microscopes have been developed that use sound waves to examine materials. These acoustic microscopes are very suitable for examining biological specimens because sound waves do not damage living tissue.

• In 1990, IBM engineers, using a scanning tunneling microscope, manipulated 35 atoms of xenon to form the letters IBM. The letters were "written" nearly a million times smaller than the type you are reading.

• Scientists at the Cavendish Laboratory, Cambridge, England, have developed an electron-beam technique for the microstorage of information. The data is reproduced as a pattern of dots on aluminum fluoride. They are able to cram up to 10 million words in each square millimeter (0.002 sq. in.).

▶ A microscope photograph showing the tubes radiating from a spiracle, or breathing hole, of a caterpillar. All insects breathe through spiracles, and the tubes carry oxygen to, and bring back carbon dioxide from, the cells in the body.

One of the smallest things our eyes can see is a pinprick. If we prick our skin with a pin, a drop of blood oozes out. We can see the drop, but not what it contains – as many as five million tiny saucerlike bodies called corpuscles. To see such bodies we need to use a microscope. We can see blood corpuscles in an optical, or light, microscope, which uses glass lenses to magnify objects. To see things that are very much smaller, such as bacteria and viruses, we must use an electron microscope, which works with a beam of electrons instead of light. Other ingenious microscopes are even able to picture atoms.

Early microscopes

Magnifying lenses made of glass came into use in the 1200s. Like modern cheap magnifying glasses, they magnified about three to five times. In the 1670s the Dutch biologist Anton van Leeuwenhoek began grinding more accurate lenses with much greater magnification (up to 300 times). With these lenses he began observing the tiny animals in pond water and even some bacteria. In so doing he helped pioneer the science of microscopy.

A few years earlier in England, the English physicist Robert Hooke had begun making observations with a compound microscope. This used two lenses to achieve a two-stage magnification. The compound principle had been discovered at the turn of the century by a Dutch eyeglass maker, Zacharias Jannsen.

The early lenses suffered from many defects, which caused progressive blurring of the image as magnification increased. The main defects were spherical and chromatic aberrations. The first was caused by the lens surface being spherical. It could be reduced by grinding the lens in a certain way. The second was caused by the glass lens acting like a prism and splitting up light into a spectrum. And the various colours were brought to a focus at different points, causing color blurring of the image. Chromatic aberration was cured in the 1830s by the use of achromatic lenses, following the practice in telescope design.

▼ This compound microscope was made by the London instrument maker Christopher Cock in the late 1600s. It has ornate decoration typical of the period.

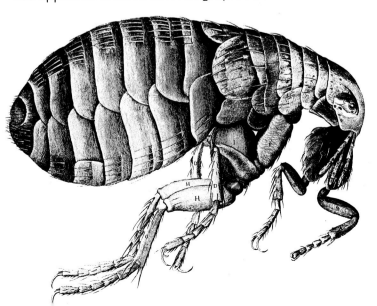

▲ The first microscope made by Anton van Leeuwenhoek in the Netherlands more than three centuries ago. It was a simple microscope. It had a single glass bead lens set between brass plates. The specimen was placed on a pointer close to the lens.

▼ Robert Hooke pioneered microscopy with a compound, or two-lens, instrument. This sketch of a flea appeared in his book *Micrographia* of 1665.

Optical microscopes

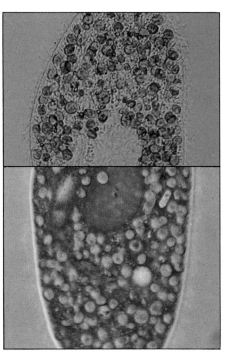

▲ Pictures of a simple invertebrate (*Paramecium bursaria*), taken at a magnification of 150 times using two different microscopes. In an ordinary microscope (top), the internal structure of the creature is indistinct. In an interference microscope (bottom), features show up much more clearly.

▲ A researcher looks through the binocular eyepiece of one of the latest microscopes. It has facilities for phase-contrast and polarized-light microscopy. It is equipped with a camera for photomicrography, and it has a screen for general viewing.

The ordinary, or optical, microscope uses two lenses, or rather combinations of lenses, to magnify an object. The magnification is done in two stages. The first magnification is brought about by a lens positioned close to the object under study. This objective lens produces a magnified, real, and upside-down image of the object. The second lens, the eyepiece, is position-ed close to the eye. It views the image and magnifies it further, producing a virtual image – one that can be seen by the eye but cannot be displayed on a screen.

The diagram shows the main features of a practical microscope. This one has a number of objective lenses mounted on a rotating turret, each with a different power of magnification. Specimens to be examined are placed on a slide, and mounted on the stage. They are often thin transparent slices of material, cut by a device called a microtome. For transparent specimens, illumination is provided from underneath by a lamp and a mirror and lens (condenser) system.

Various techniques are used in microscopy to bring out details in a specimen. Many biological materials are stained by dyes to make their structure stand out. Some are dyed with fluorescent substances, which show up when they are illuminated with ultraviolet light. Fluorescence microscopy has proved valuable in medical research, where it has been used, for example, to identify chromosomes.

Some rocks and minerals are examined under ultraviolet light because they fluoresce natural-ly. In a petrographic microscope they are examined in polarized light, which is light that vibrates in only one plane. Using this technique, crystals in a rock that look much the same in ordinary light appear quite different and often brilliantly colored in polarized light.

Another technique used in research work to bring out details in an image is phase-contrast microscopy. It does not involve staining or other techniques that could harm living things, so it can be used to record such events as cell division. The phase-contrast microscope exploits the fact that different parts of a specimen slow down light passing through them by differing amounts. This results in a difference in phase between the light waves. In other words, they get out of step and interfere with one another. The result is a pattern of light and dark, which emphasizes details of structure. The interference microscope works on the same principle.

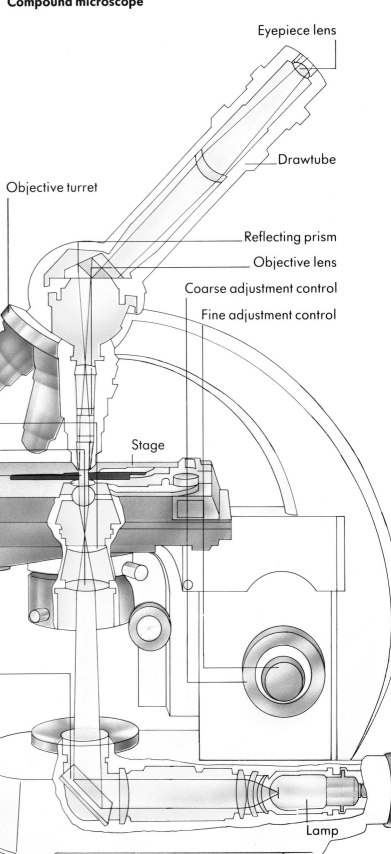

Compound microscope

Eyepiece lens

Drawtube

Objective turret

Reflecting prism

Objective lens

Coarse adjustment control

Fine adjustment control

Condenser

Auxiliary lens

Specimen

Stage

Mirror

Lamp

▲ Rock crystals can be studied under a microscope in ordinary light (top), but show up better in polarized light (bottom).

▶ The main features of a compound microscope. The optical system below the stage provides even illumination of the specimen. The objective forms a magnified image, which the eyepiece then views, via a reflecting prism.

21

Electron microscopes

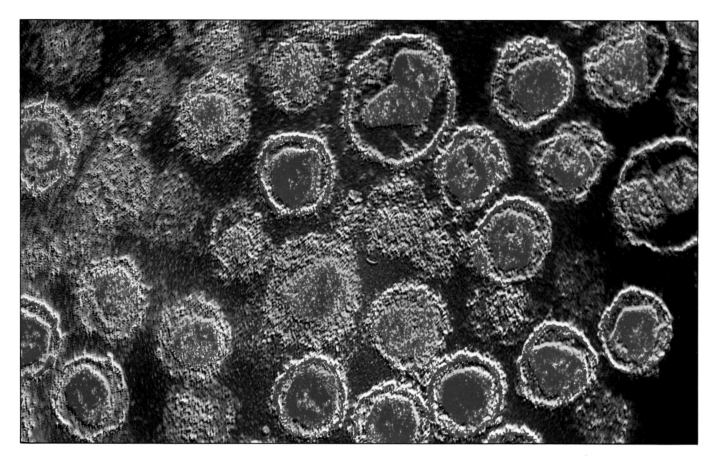

The most powerful ordinary microscopes can resolve, or show as separate, objects that are up to about 200 millionths of a millimeter (8 millionths of an inch) apart. They can magnify up to about 2,500 times. Their resolving power, or resolution, is limited by the length of the light wave – it is too big a yardstick.

The shorter the wavelength used, the greater is the resolution. So using shorter-wavelength ultraviolet light, for example, twice the resolution (100 millionths of a millimeter) is possible. But for very much higher resolution, we must abandon light and turn to the electron.

Electrons, when they are produced in a beam, behave like a wave motion. And it is a wave motion with very short wavelengths indeed – down to less than one-millionth of a millimeter.

Experiments in using an electron beam to create a high-resolution microscope began in the early 1930s. And the first practical electron microscope appeared in 1936. Since then many developments have taken place, which now allow scientists to achieve magnifications of one million times or more.

The original type of electron microscope is the transmission electron microscope (TEM). The essential features of the instrument are shown in the diagram. It uses an electron "gun" to produce a beam of electrons. A series of magnetic "lenses" focus the beam and form a magnified image after it passes through a specimen. They act like the objective and eyepiece lenses of an optical microscope. Finally, the beam holding the magnified image is projected on a fluorescent screen, which makes the image visible. This can be viewed through a binocular eyepiece, or photographed.

The scanning electron microscope (SEM) produces images by scanning the surface of a specimen in a series of lines with a fine electron beam. Where the beam strikes it, the surface gives off secondary electrons. The pattern of electrons given off holds an image of the surface. These electrons are collected, line by line, and form the brightness signals for a beam scanning in a cathode-ray tube. An image is built up on the screen, line by line, in much the same way as a television picture is made.

◄ This is a picture of viruses that cause cancer in birds, taken in a transmission electron microscope. False colors have been added to make the virus particles (red) stand out. Viruses are so tiny that they can be seen only in electron microscopes, which can provide magnifications of a million times or more.

► Features of a transmission electron microscope (TEM). The main body consists of a column from which the air has been removed. An electron beam is produced at the top of the column by an electron gun, similar to that in a cathode-ray tube. At intervals lower down are sets of magnetic coils, which act as lenses to focus the beam and direct it through a thin slice of specimen. The beam that emerges carries an image of the specimen, which is magnified by another set of lenses (objective). A final set of lenses projects the magnified electron image onto a fluorescent screen, where it becomes visible, and can be photographed.

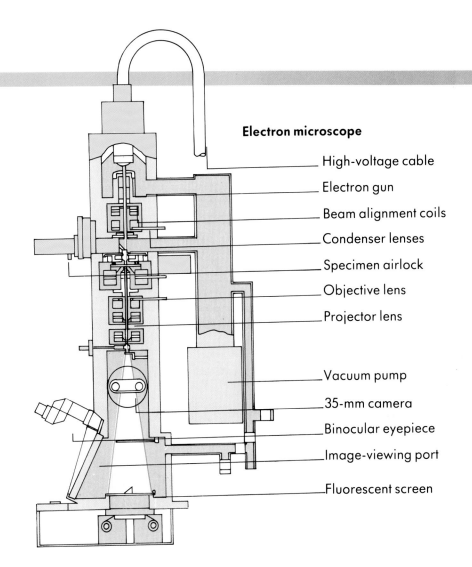

Electron microscope

High-voltage cable
Electron gun
Beam alignment coils
Condenser lenses
Specimen airlock
Objective lens
Projector lens

Vacuum pump
35-mm camera
Binocular eyepiece
Image-viewing port
Fluorescent screen

◄ A bird cherry aphid next to the exoskeleton it has just cast off, pictured by a scanning electron microscope (SEM). Vivid three-dimensional images like this make the SEM one of the most fascinating tools in scientific and medical research.

▼ A researcher at the operating console of an SEM. In the instrument the specimen is scanned by a pencil-thin electron beam.

Seeing far

► Telescope domes at Kitt Peak Observatory in Arizona. The largest dome houses the Mayall reflector, which has a light-gathering mirror 4 m (158 in.) in diameter.

Just as they cannot easily see very tiny objects, our eyes cannot easily see very distant or very faint objects, such as the heavenly bodies. To see such objects more clearly, we must use telescopes, whose lenses or mirrors can gather more light than our eyes.

Using powerful telescopes and a variety of other instruments, astronomers can tell us what stars are made of and how they live and die. Astronomers also build telescopes to collect radio waves from the heavens, and send telescopes into space on satellites to observe our mysterious Universe at other wavelengths as well.

Early telescopes

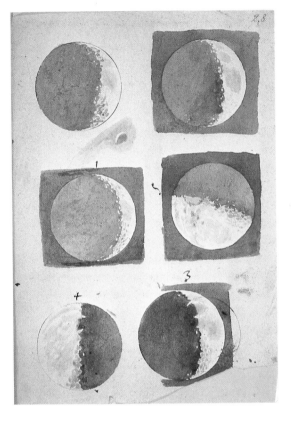

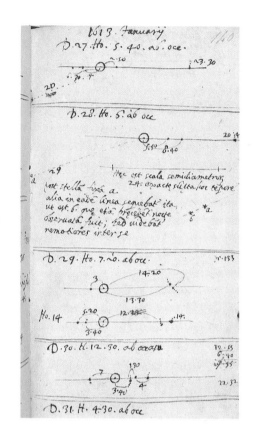

The birth of modern astronomy, the scientific study of the heavens, can be dated at 1609. In the winter of that year in Padua, Italy, a professor of mathematics, Galileo Galilei, made a telescope and trained it on the heavens. He became the first person to see the mountains on the Moon, the four large moons of Jupiter, and the phases of Venus. His observations helped convince him and other astronomers that the Sun and not the Earth was the center of our planetary system.

Galileo's telescope used a pair of lenses to gather light and produce a magnified view of the heavenly bodies. It was a type called a refractor, because the path of light was refracted, or bent, as it passed through the lenses.

The early refractors, however, suffered from several defects, which blurred the image. To improve image quality, the English scientist Isaac Newton in 1668 built a telescope that used a concave (dish-shaped) mirror to gather and focus light. This type of telescope, called a reflector, is the one used mostly by astronomers today. But whereas the early reflectors were made of polished metal, the modern ones are made of glass coated with aluminum.

▲▶ Galileo pioneered astronomy through the telescope, leaving sketches and detailed notes. These two telescopes of his (right) have magnifications of 14 and 20.

▼ Isaac Newton's reflecting telescope of 1668 was a great advance because it did not suffer from lens defects.

Refractors and reflectors

Refractors

These days lens-type, or refracting, telescopes are still widely used by amateur astronomers. In small sizes, they can give excellent results. A refractor uses two lenses to form an image – an objective and an eyepiece. The objective is a converging lens, or rather lens combination, which has a long focal length. It gathers the light from a distant object and forms an image. The eyepiece, which is also a converging lens, views and magnifies the image. The objective is mounted at the front of the main telescope tube, while the eyepiece is mounted in a tube that can slide in and out of the main one to bring the image into sharp focus.

Refractors suffer from two main optical defects, or aberrations, which cause blurred images. One is spherical aberration, which results from the lens having slightly the wrong curvature. This defect is reduced by grinding the lens into shape with the utmost accuracy. The other main lens defect is chromatic (color) aberration. This is a color blurring of the image caused by the lens refracting light of different wavelengths (colors) by slightly different amounts. This defect is corrected by using achromatic lenses.

Refractors are difficult to make in large sizes because of the way they are constructed. They can be supported only around the edge. Large lenses are heavy and difficult to mount in this way without being distorted. The largest refractor, at Yerkes Observatory in Wisconsin, has a lens only 100 cm (40 in.) across.

Reflectors

Mirror-type telescopes, or reflectors, do not suffer from chromatic aberration. Also, they can be made in much larger sizes because their mirrors can be supported from behind, which prevents distortion. As a result, reflectors can be built with mirrors several meters across. The world's largest single-mirror telescope has a mirror 6 m (236 in.) across. It is sited near Zelenchuk-skaya, in the Caucasus Mountains, Russia. However, this massive reflector is optically not as flexible in use as smaller modern instruments, such as the 4.2-m (165-in.)

▲ This refractor has an objective lens 10 cm (4 in.) in diameter, a popular size with amateur astronomers. It carries a "finder," a small telescope to help locate the target object. It is mounted on a sturdy tripod.

▶ The Mayall 4-m (158-in) reflector at Kitt Peak National Observatory in Arizona. The telescope is moved bodily to follow the motion of the stars by rotation of the horseshoe bearing, visible here.

▲ This is another Kitt Peak instrument, a Schmidt reflector with a 91-cm (36-in.) diameter mirror. The Schmidt telescope is designed to have a wide field of view. It has a mirror with spherical curvature, which focuses light on a photographic plate. A specially shaped lens is placed in the mouth of the telescope tube to ensure that light reflected from every point on the mirror is brought sharply into focus.

William Herschel reflector. This telescope, at the Roque de los Muchachos Observatory on La Palma in the Canary Islands, uses superior optics and advanced computer control and electronic instrumentation. It could detect the light of a candle 150,000 km (93,000 mi.) away.

There are several kinds of reflectors, which gather and focus incoming starlight in different ways. They all have a concave primary mirror to gather the light. This mirror may focus an image directly on a photographic plate at the so-called prime-focus position. Or it may reflect the light to another mirror. This secondary mirror may in turn reflect the light into a viewing eyepiece at the side (Newtonian focus) or back down the telescope tube and through a hole in the primary mirror (Cassegrain focus).

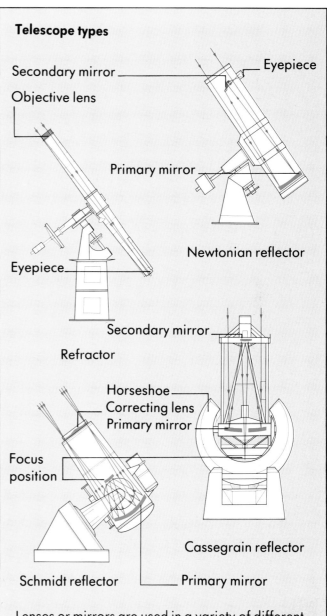

Telescope types

Secondary mirror
Objective lens
Eyepiece
Primary mirror
Newtonian reflector
Eyepiece
Refractor
Secondary mirror
Horseshoe
Correcting lens
Primary mirror
Focus position
Cassegrain reflector
Schmidt reflector
Primary mirror

Lenses or mirrors are used in a variety of different combinations in telescopes to gather and focus the faint light from the stars. A refractor uses two sets of lenses (objective and eyepiece) to gather the light and view the image. In the Newtonian type of reflector, light gathered by the primary mirror is further reflected by a plane secondary mirror into an eyepiece in the side of the telescope tube. In a Cassegrain reflector, a curved secondary mirror reflects light back down the telescope tube through a hole in the primary mirror. A Schmidt reflector uses a correcting lens in the telescope tube to ensure sharp focusing by its spherical mirror. It provides a wide-angle view of the heavens.

Astronomical observatories

Astronomical observatories, where astronomers carry out their observations, must be sited to avoid conditions that make for bad viewing. Most are located far from city lights high up on mountain tops, where the air is still and clear and the climate is dry. Among well-known mountain-top observatories are the Palomar Observatory on Mt Palomar in California and Kitt Peak National Observatory in Arizona; Siding Spring Observatory in New South Wales, Australia; and Roque de los Muchachos Observatory on La Palma, in the Canary Islands.

Mounting and recording

Telescopes are housed in dome-shaped buildings, whose roofs slide back at night to expose the telescopes to the stars. The telescopes are controlled, nowadays by computer, so that they can point to any part of the sky.

▲ One of the newest and finest observatories, the Roque de los Muchachos Observatory on La Palma, in the Canary Islands. It is located at an altitude of 2,250 m (7,700 ft.), where it is above the cloud base and where the skies are nearly always crystal clear.

▼ The world's largest solar telescope, the McMath, forms part of the extensive telescope complex at Kitt Peak National Observatory. A mirror (heliostat) reflects sunlight down a sloping shaft 153 m (500 ft.) long. Other mirrors reflect and focus it into an image.

▶ Stars trail in circular arcs around the north celestial pole in this long-exposure photograph taken at the Roque de los Muchachos Observatory in the Canary Islands. The two telescopes here are the 1-m (40-in.) Jacobus Kapteyn and the 2.5-m (98-in.) Isaac Newton telescopes. The latter was originally located at the Royal Greenwich Observatory in Sussex, England.

▼ An astronomer works at the operating console of the 3.9-m (153-in.) Anglo-Australian telescope at the Siding Spring Observatory in New South Wales. One of the most powerful instruments in the Southern Hemisphere, the telescope is under computer control.

Because the Earth spins on its axis, the stars appear to move through the heavens. So, to follow a particular star for any length of time, the telescope must also move. This is most simply done if the telescope has an equatorial mounting. This has one axis of movement parallel with the Earth's axis. The telescope is then rotated around this axis at the same speed the Earth (and the star) is moving.

Astronomers use their large telescopes as giant cameras and record images on photographic film. This is done because film is more sensitive than the eye and can store light. And the longer it is exposed, the more light it stores, which enables it to record very faint stars and galaxies. Light coming through the telescope is also analyzed, notably in spectroscopes, which split it into a spectrum. By studying the spectrum, astronomers can discover a remarkable amount of information about the star the light came from, including its composition, temperature, and speed.

In recent years electronic methods of light detection have come into use, which are more sensitive than photographic film. They include such devices as charge-coupled devices (CCDs). These are silicon chips that are light-sensitive. The pattern of incoming light produces on the chip a pattern of charges, which a computer can convert into a visible image.

Radio telescopes

▲ The distinctive Whirlpool galaxy, pictured by the Very Large Array radio telescope near Socorro, New Mexico. The picture was obtained by converting the pattern of radio signals emitted by the galaxy into an image on a computer screen. The colors show variations in the strength of emission: red is highest, purple lowest.

◄ Some of the 27 antennas of the Very Large Array. They can be arranged in different positions along a Y-shaped track. Each antenna has a dish 25 m (82 ft.) in diameter.

Visible light is not the only means by which stars give off energy. Stars give off many other kinds of radiation as well, such as gamma rays, X-rays, ultraviolet rays, infrared rays, and radio waves. Like visible light, these are all electromagnetic waves. They differ only in their wavelength, some having a shorter wavelength, and others a longer wavelength, than visible light. Most of these radiations are blocked by the atmosphere. Radio waves, however, can get through.

Radio waves were first detected coming from the heavens in 1931. Since that time radio astronomy has grown into one of the most exciting branches of astronomy. It has led to the discovery of hyperactive galaxies that pour out millions of times more energy than normal; pulsating stars made out of neutrons; and mysterious quasars, bodies that are hundreds of times brighter than galaxies but millions of times smaller.

Radio telescopes are quite unlike optical telescopes. Some consist of long arrays of wire antennas, and are fixed to the ground. Others are giant dishes, which can be steered to point to different parts of the sky. The dishes act as

reflectors to gather the very faint waves and focus them on a central receiving antenna. Electronic circuits then amplify (strengthen) the incoming signals, which are converted into images by computer.

Two of the largest steerable radio telescopes are at Jodrell Bank (76-m, or 250-ft., diameter) in Cheshire, England, and at Effelsberg (100-m, or 328-ft., diameter), near Bonn, Germany. The biggest dish, however, is fixed. It is made of aluminum mesh and suspended in a natural bowl in hills near Arecibo, in Puerto Rico. It measures 305 m (1,000 ft.) across. It is used not only in passive mode as a receiving telescope, but also in active mode for radar observations of the nearer planets. It beams signals to a planet and records the "echoes," or reflected signals. In this way it can build up a picture of the planet's surface, which in the case of Venus is permanently hidden by layers of cloud.

Some radio telescopes use several dishes working in concert, a technique called aperture synthesis. Moving the dishes into different positions gives the same results as one very large dish would. Telescopes in different parts of the Earth can be linked in this way.

▲ American radio engineer Karl Jansky, and the antenna with which he discovered radio waves coming from the heavens. At the time, 1931, Jansky was investigating the source of interference in radio transmissions for Bell Telephone Laboratories. In pinpointing the source as outer space, he launched the science of radio astronomy. In 1937 another American, Grote Reber, built a 9.5-m (31-ft.) dish reflector to gather radio waves, pioneering the most common type of radio telescope today.

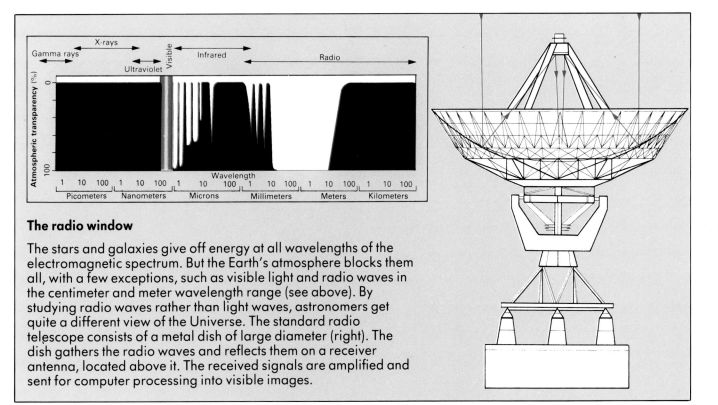

The radio window

The stars and galaxies give off energy at all wavelengths of the electromagnetic spectrum. But the Earth's atmosphere blocks them all, with a few exceptions, such as visible light and radio waves in the centimeter and meter wavelength range (see above). By studying radio waves rather than light waves, astronomers get quite a different view of the Universe. The standard radio telescope consists of a metal dish of large diameter (right). The dish gathers the radio waves and reflects them on a receiver antenna, located above it. The received signals are amplified and sent for computer processing into visible images.

Space telescopes

When the Space Age got into its stride in the 1960s, space scientists began sending instruments into orbit on satellites. Astronomers were not slow to take advantage of this new technology. On Earth their vision of the Universe is distorted by the dust, moisture and air currents in the atmosphere. Sending their telescopes, detectors, and other instruments

▼ The *Einstein Observatory* was an astronomy satellite designed to record X-rays from the heavens. It had a "grazing incidence" telescope, which focused the X-rays by reflecting them through shallow angles. At bottom is an image obtained from *Einstein* of powerful X-ray sources in the Eta Carinae nebula.

into space on satellites enabled them to view the Universe more clearly. They were also able to view it at wavelengths the atmosphere absorbs: gamma-ray, X-ray, ultraviolet, and infrared. Viewed at these other wavelengths, the Universe looked quite different from what it did in visible light. The study of X-rays from the heavens began in the 1960s with instruments carried into the high atmosphere by rockets. X-ray detectors were included on Orbiting Astronomical Observatories launched in 1968 and 1972. *OAO 3*, named *Copernicus*, was particularly successful. Later satellites, such as *Exosat* (1983), mapped the X-ray sky. They

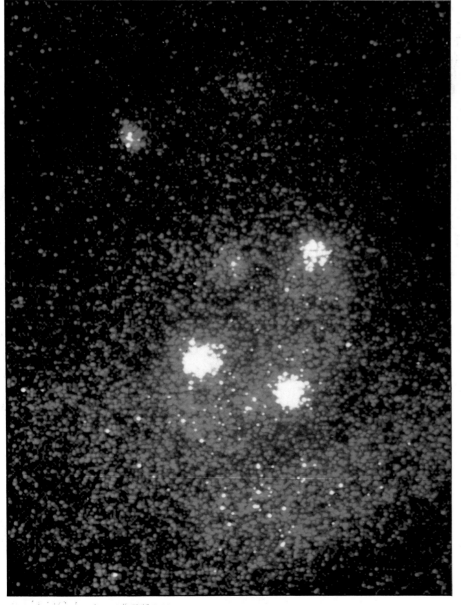

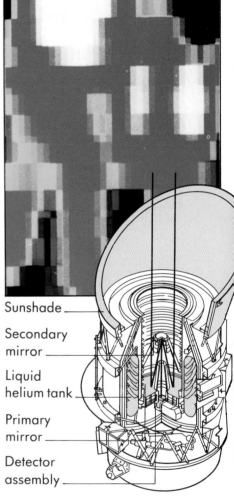

Sunshade

Secondary mirror

Liquid helium tank

Primary mirror

Detector assembly

▲ *IRAS*, the *Infrared Astronomy Satellite*. To make it sensitive to incoming infrared rays, the detector was cooled by liquid helium to −269°C (−452°F). At the top is an *IRAS* image of the Tarantula nebula.

found evidence of the presence of those awesome bodies we know as black holes, which gobble up everything nearby, even light.

From the early 1960s numerous satellites carried instruments to detect gamma rays. The first startling gamma-ray discoveries were made in 1967 by U.S. atomic scientists using spy satellites to look for gamma rays from nuclear-bomb tests on Earth. Instead, they detected bursts of gamma rays from the heavens. These lasted only a fraction of a second, but packed the power of 100,000 Suns. They became known as bursters.

Exploration of the wavelengths on either side of the visible spectrum, the ultraviolet and infrared, has been revolutionized by two satellites. One is the *International Ultraviolet Explorer* (*IUE*), still working in 1990 after 12 years in orbit. The other was the *Infrared Astronomy Satellite* (*IRAS*), which worked for 10 months in 1983.

In 1990 the Hubble Space Telescope (HST) was launched into orbit to pioneer optical astronomy from space. Amazingly, once in orbit, its main light-gathering mirror was found to be defective, and the hoped-for quantum leap in optical performance over Earth-based telescopes did not happen.

▼ The Hubble Space Telescope, launched from the Space Shuttle in April 1990, gathers light with a 2.4-m (94-in.) diameter mirror. Despite a mirror flaw it has still managed to acquire good images, including the first clear picture showing Pluto's moon Charon.

Aperture door

Secondary mirror

Radio antenna

Stray-light baffles

Central baffle

Instrument package

Primary mirror

Guidance sensors

Solar panel

▼ An HST image showing the ring around the supernova star 1987A.

Analyzing and probing

Spot facts

Spot facts

• By using a combination of gas chromatography (for separation) and mass spectroscopy (for analysis), chemists can identify substances in a mixture present in concentrations as low as one part per million.

• The latest echo sounders, using sound waves vibrating up to 10 million times a second, can pick out individual fish in a school.

• In experiments with atom smashers, nuclear physicists have discovered hundreds of subatomic particles, each with an equivalent antiparticle.

• In the latest atom smashers, colliding beams of particles create tiny fireballs that are hundreds of millions of times hotter than the Sun.

▶ A shower of subatomic particles, produced in a bubble chamber at CERN, Europe's nuclear research center in Geneva, Switzerland. Some were created by smashing together high-speed particles in a particle accelerator. Others are cosmic rays, which reach the Earth from outer space.

Scientists and engineers use both traditional and modern methods to investigate the makeup of materials, the way these materials behave, and the processes they undergo. Chemists, for example, still mix chemicals in test tubes, but also analyze substances with advanced instruments like mass spectrographs. They also use radiation methods in analysis, while engineers use them to examine materials for hidden flaws. Nuclear physicists use the biggest and most expensive scientific equipment of all – particle accelerators, or atom smashers – to help them probe into the very heart of the atom.

Research

Our knowledge of science, along with our ability to apply that science to create useful machines and devices, is the product of centuries of inspiration and perspiration by legions of dedicated scientists and inventors.

The first systematic scientific exploration, or research, into the nature of matter was carried out by the ancient alchemists. They flourished in the Middle Ages, trying to find a method of turning base metals into gold. Although they failed in their attempts, they made discoveries that laid the foundations of chemical science.

Modern science has its origins in the 1600s and 1700s, when the likes of Isaac Newton in England and Galileo in Italy established fundamental physical laws, and Robert Boyle in England and Antoine Lavoisier in France expanded chemical knowledge. All these early scientists conducted what is often called pure research – investigation for its own sake, without a particular goal in mind.

But as the chemical industry began to expand in the late 1700s, scientists began to direct their research along more practical lines. Such applied research led, for example, to the French chemist Nicholas Leblanc developing a process for converting salt into soda ash (sodium carbonate). This was much in demand for the manufacture of soap and glass. Sometimes research in one direction led by chance to another. For example, while trying to synthesize the drug quinine, the English chemist William H. Perkin in 1856 discovered the brilliant coal-tar dyes, and launched a whole new industry.

These days scientific research is usually a team effort and linked with specific industries. The prolific American inventor Thomas A. Edison set up one of the first dedicated research laboratories in New Jersey in the 1870s.

◄▲ The changing face of the chemical research laboratory, from the 1840s to the present day. The test tubes and gas burners of the past have long since disappeared. In today's laboratories chemicals are often analyzed automatically by electronic instruments, and the results are calculated and displayed by a computer.

Chemical analysis

The analysis of chemical substances is bread-and-butter work to the laboratory chemist. It is routinely carried out, for example, to test for the purity of food, drugs, and water supplies, and to check the progress of chemical processes in industry. Chemists carry out both qualitative analysis, to identify which substances are present, and quantitative analysis, to measure the amount of those substances.

The substances chemists have to deal with are usually mixtures, and some form of separation is required before components can be identified. Physical methods of separation may be possible, which involve such processes as filtration, distillation, and centrifuging. These make use of physical differences between the components, such as in their boiling point. Chemical separation may be possible: a chemical reagent may be added so as to cause a substance to precipitate.

A much more sensitive and quicker method of separation is chromatography. This relies on the varying degrees of attraction different kinds of molecules have for an inert substance. In paper chromatography, for example, a strip of paper forms the inert substance (the stationary phase). A drop of solution of the mixture to be analyzed is placed on the paper, which is then dipped in a suitable solvent. This is called the mobile phase, because it moves along the paper. It carries with it the components in the mixture. But these are attracted to differing extents by the paper, so they travel at different speeds and gradually separate out.

In gas chromatograpy, an inert gas such as

▼ An industrial chemist uses an electronic instrument called a coulometer to test the moisture content of plastic roofing material. Her colleague is examining another sample under a microscope. Electronic instruments are now standard laboratory equipment.

Spectroscopic analysis

When white light is passed through a prism, it is split up into a spectrum: a spread of different colors, or wavelengths. When chemical elements are excited, or given excess energy, their atoms afterward lose energy by giving out light. If this light is split into a spectrum, bright lines are seen at different wavelengths. This is called a bright-line, or emission, spectrum. Each element has a characteristic emission spectrum, so this method can be used in analysis.

Elements also absorb certain wavelengths. When light is passed through a sample and split into a spectrum, dark lines show up at different wavelengths. This absorption, or dark-line, spectrum, is again characteristic of the elements present.

Other spectroscopic methods are used to study the makeup of crystals and molecules. X-ray diffraction spectroscopy uses the way X-rays are scattered by atoms. Nuclear magnetic resonance (NMR) spectroscopy uses radio waves in the presence of a strong magnetic field.

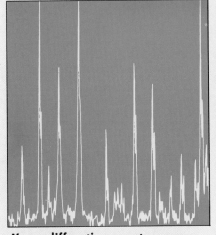

Emission spectroscopy

Absorption spectroscopy

X-ray diffraction spectroscopy

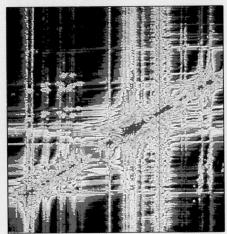

NMR spectroscopy

nitrogen is the mobile phase. It carries a vaporized sample of the mixture through a column packed with material coated with a suitable liquid (stationary phase). The components separated by this method may be identified by the time they take to pass through the column, or by mass spectroscopy. This method works by ionizing the components and then identifying them by their mass and electric charge. It is one of several spectroscopic methods now widely used. These rely on the fact that atoms and molecules display a characteristic spectrum as they absorb energy or give it off when in a high-energy state.

▶ Children in a school laboratory observe the changes that have occurred in a solution after a chemical experiment.

Radiation methods

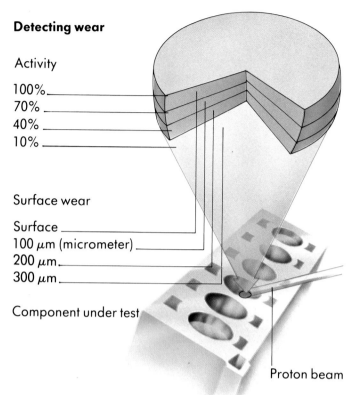

Detecting wear

Activity

100% ——
70% ——
40% ——
10% ——

Surface wear

Surface ——
100 μm (micrometer) ——
200 μm ——
300 μm ——

Component under test

Proton beam

The visual inspection of materials and structures plays a vital role in many branches of industry. And over the years engineers have come up with ingenious devices, such as endoscopes, to peer into places the eye cannot see. The doctor, too, uses such devices to peer inside the body and even carry out operations there.

However, these devices give only limited information. They cannot see internal flaws in materials, or abnormalities in body tissues. The engineer and doctor therefore resort to methods employing radiation that can penetrate materials and flesh. And by means of photography or imagery generated by computers, they can produce pictures showing internal details. Such study is called radiography.

The first kind of radiation used was X-rays, a short-wavelength electromagnetic radiation discovered by the German physicist Wilhelm Roentgen in 1895. X-rays are produced when a

▲▼ The amount of wear in, say, an engine cylinder can be checked by what is called thin-layer activation. The surface of the metal in the bore is covered with a radioactive layer. Later the radioactivity of the layer is measured with a radiation detector. A reduction in the level of activity will indicate that wear of the metal in the bore has taken place.

material (usually tungsten) is bombarded by high-energy particles (usually electrons). To make a radiograph, X-rays are sent through the subject under examination on to a photographic plate. A shadow image is produced when different parts of the internal structures absorb different amounts of radiation.

In medicine, the simple X-ray technique can show bones, but not delicate tissues or details of internal organs. In the 1970s a much more sensitive method came into use which can. It is called computed tomography, or computer-assisted tomography (CAT). It images a "slice" of the body with an X-ray source in a rotating frame. As the source rotates, sensitive detectors beneath the body measure the amount of radiation passing through. A computer analyses the readings and converts them into an image on a video screen.

Engineers now also use gamma rays for materials testing; they are even more penetrating than X-rays. Artificial radioactive isotopes, or radioisotopes, are the source of these rays. Since they are readily portable, they can be used anywhere, unlike X-ray equipment.

Radioisotopes are also useful in medical research and even for treatment. Research scientists use them as tracers, for example, to follow the blood flow through the brain. Their progress can be traced by means of radiation detectors, such as the Geiger counter.

Radioisotopes are also used to reveal how particular substances are taken up by the body. For example, iodine naturally accumulates in the thyroid gland. To check how the thyroid is working, doctors inject the patient with radioactive iodine. They can then monitor, with radiation detectors, how the gland handles the iodine, and this will tell them whether the thyroid is working normally or not.

X-ray tube

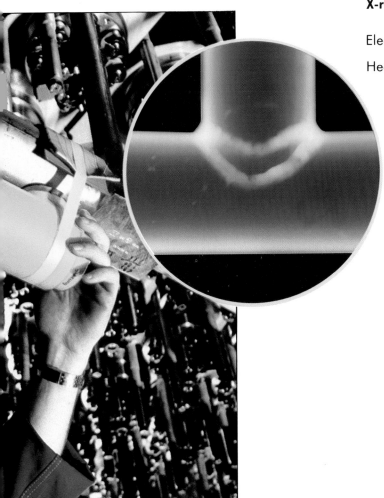

Electron beam

Heated cathode

Emitted X-rays

Cooled tungsten anode

▲ X-rays are produced in a vacuum tube like this. A stream of electrons from the heated cathode is accelerated by a high voltage and strikes the tungsten anode. The atoms in the metal become highly energized, and give out their excess energy in the form of X-rays. The process generates heat, so the anode has to be cooled. This may be done by means of a liquid coolant, as here, or by rotating the anode. X-rays have wavelengths between about 10 picometers (trillonths of a meter) and about 1 nanometer (billionth of a meter).

◄ Inspecting welds on a pipeline at a nuclear power plant with X-ray equipment. The X-rays penetrate the metal and clearly show up any defects there might be in the welds. The inset radiograph shows a flaw.

Sound methods

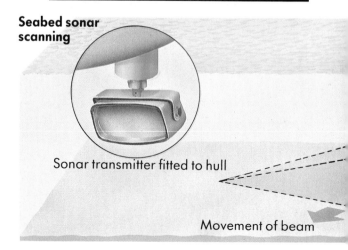

Seabed sonar scanning

Sonar transmitter fitted to hull

Movement of beam

Scientists, engineers, and doctors do not use just electromagnetic waves to examine internal structures, they also use sound waves. We normally think of sound as traveling only through air. But in fact it can travel through all kinds of materials, such as water, glass, rock, and steel. Indeed it travels much faster in these materials than in air. Whereas in air the speed of sound is only about 1,200 km/h (750 mph), in water it is more than four times faster, and in steel it is nearly four times faster still.

Instruments employing sound for detection are useful for probing the atmosphere, the oceans, the Earth, and the human body. All these instruments work by sending out sound waves and "listening" for reflections, or echoes. They are often called echo sounders.

Meteorologists may use echo sounding in the atmosphere to measure levels of humidity, or to detect where there are temperature inversions, atmospheric conditions likely to give rise to pollution. Geologists use echo-sounding techniques to study underground rock layers. This procedure is called seismic surveying.

At sea, echo sounders are used by ships' navigators to measure water depth and by fisherman to locate schools of fish. They are also used as underwater radar to scan the depths for wrecks and rocks and, on naval ships, for submarines. This method of underwater echolocation is generally known as sonar (sound navigation and ranging).

The sound waves used for sonar are generally of very high frequency. These are too high-pitched to be heard by the human ear, and are termed ultrasonic. The ear can hear sounds only up to a frequency of about 20,000 hertz (cycles per second). But sonar uses frequencies of up to 10 megahertz (million hertz).

Ultrasonic frequencies are also used for probing inside materials. The reflections, or echoes, of internal structures are computer-processed to provide an image. This is a valuable method of nondestructive testing in engineering, useful for detecting flaws in welds, for example. In medicine a similar technique is used to image the fetus in a mother's womb.

◀ Engineers checking welds in high-pressure water pipes during the construction of the Dinorwic hydroelectric power plant in Wales. They are using an ultrasonic probe, linked with a computer. Flaws in the welds show up clearly on the computer screen. In the inset computer image, the flaw is the large red spot below center.

▼▶ Ultrasound is also used in sonar methods of underwater detection. The survey ship shown in the diagram below is scanning forward and sideways over the seabed as it travels. Echoes received back are processed by computer to form an image of anything on the seabed, such as a wreck. The image can be displayed in false color, as here (right). It even shows the acoustic "shadow" made by the vessel.

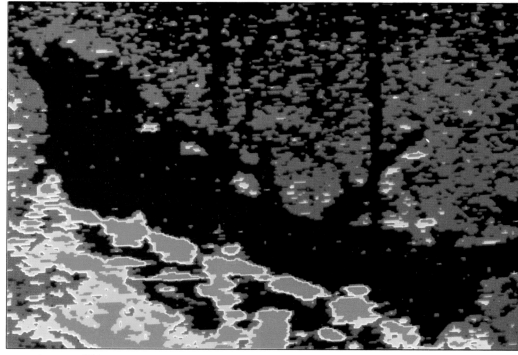

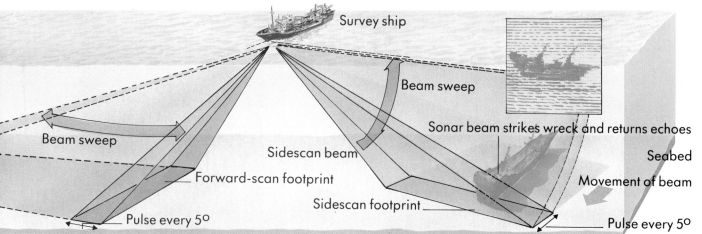

Survey ship

Beam sweep

Beam sweep

Sidescan beam

Forward-scan footprint

Sidescan footprint

Pulse every 5°

Sonar beam strikes wreck and returns echoes

Seabed

Movement of beam

Pulse every 5°

Laser methods

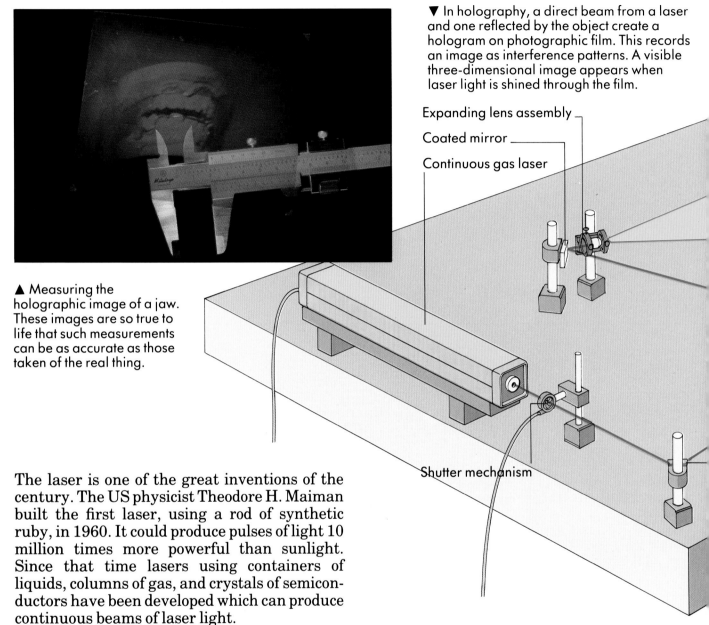

▼ In holography, a direct beam from a laser and one reflected by the object create a hologram on photographic film. This records an image as interference patterns. A visible three-dimensional image appears when laser light is shined through the film.

Expanding lens assembly

Coated mirror

Continuous gas laser

Shutter mechanism

▲ Measuring the holographic image of a jaw. These images are so true to life that such measurements can be as accurate as those taken of the real thing.

The laser is one of the great inventions of the century. The US physicist Theodore H. Maiman built the first laser, using a rod of synthetic ruby, in 1960. It could produce pulses of light 10 million times more powerful than sunlight. Since that time lasers using containers of liquids, columns of gas, and crystals of semiconductors have been developed which can produce continuous beams of laser light.

The term laser stands for "light amplification by stimulated emission of radiation," which explains how it works. Atoms in the laser medium (gas, liquid, or solid) are "excited," or forced into a high-energy state. Some spontaneously emit the extra energy as light radiation of a particular wavelength, or color. This radiation triggers, or stimulates, other atoms to emit light of the same wavelength, which in turn stimulates still other atoms. In this way the radiation increases rapidly in strength. The laser has parallel mirrors at each end so that the radiation is reflected to and fro, stimulating emission from more atoms each time. One of the mirrors allows the radiation to emerge as an intense beam of parallel rays.

Laser light is special for three main reasons. One, it is very pure, being very nearly a single color, or wavelength. Two, laser light is coherent, which means that all its waves are exactly in step with one another. This means that they reinforce one another and build up energy. The waves of ordinary light are out of step with one another, which makes them, as it were, jostle one another and lose energy. Three, laser light is highly directional, being produced in a beam of almost perfectly parallel rays.

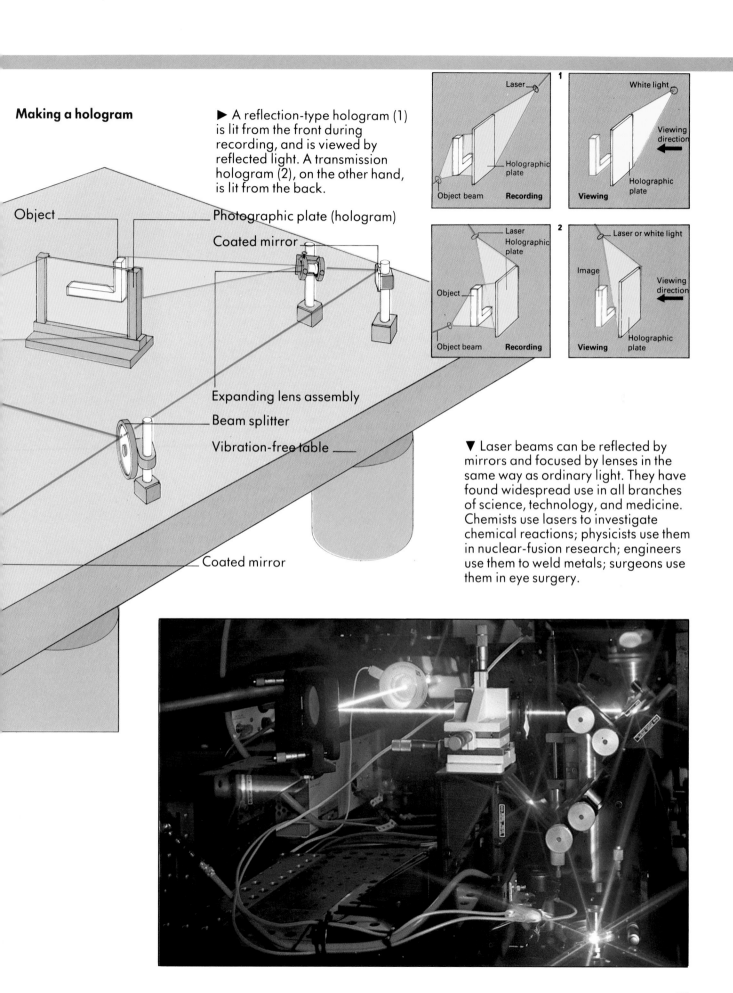

Making a hologram

▶ A reflection-type hologram (1) is lit from the front during recording, and is viewed by reflected light. A transmission hologram (2), on the other hand, is lit from the back.

Object

Photographic plate (hologram)

Coated mirror

Expanding lens assembly

Beam splitter

Vibration-free table

Coated mirror

1

Laser

Holographic plate

Object beam **Recording**

White light

Viewing direction

Holographic plate

Viewing

2

Laser

Holographic plate

Object

Object beam **Recording**

Laser or white light

Image

Viewing direction

Holographic plate

Viewing

▼ Laser beams can be reflected by mirrors and focused by lenses in the same way as ordinary light. They have found widespread use in all branches of science, technology, and medicine. Chemists use lasers to investigate chemical reactions; physicists use them in nuclear-fusion research; engineers use them to weld metals; surgeons use them in eye surgery.

Atom smashing

Underneath the fields just outside Geneva, in Switzerland, lies the largest scientific instrument in the world. It explores the smallest piece of ordinary matter in the world – the atom. It was built by CERN, the European Laboratory for Particle Physics.

The instrument is a particle accelerator, popularly called an atom smasher. It occupies a ring-shaped tunnel 27 km (17 mi.) in circumference and on average more than 100 m (300 ft.) underground. Inside a pipe within the tunnel two streams of charged particles are accelerated in opposite directions and then made to collide. The collision produces a shower of other particles, which are recorded by a detector, such as a bubble chamber.

This atom smasher produces collisions between beams of negatively charged electrons and their antiparticles, positively charged positrons. Other powerful atom smashers of similar design, such as the Tevatron at Fermilab, near Chicago, collide beams of protons and antiprotons.

These great atomic "race tracks" using colliding beams were developed from accelerators known as synchrotrons. These use electric fields to repel and thus accelerate a beam of charged particles in a rhythmic (synchronized) way, giving them a little "push" on every circuit. The beam is deflected into a circular path by means of thousands of electromagnets. Other accelerators acccelerate particles in a straight line. The Stanford linear collider in California, for example, accelerates particles down a long tunnel 3.2 km (2 mi.) long.

▼ An aerial view of Fermilab's giant synchrotron, the Tevatron, near Chicago, which has been operating since 1983. The tunnels in which particles are accelerated to high energies are located underground. They measure 6.3 km (3.8 mi.) in circumference.

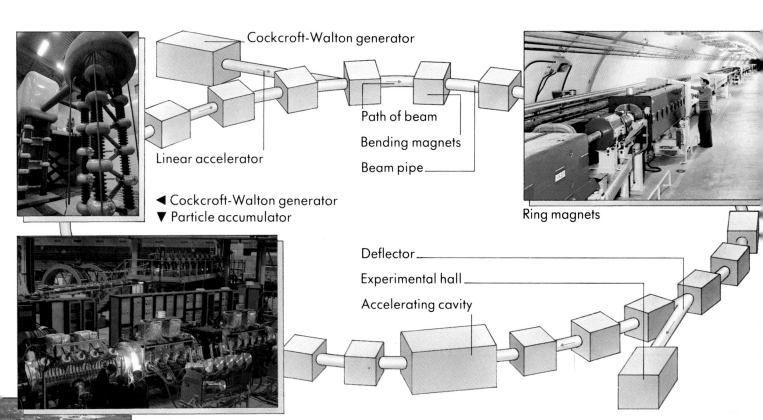

Cockcroft-Walton generator

Linear accelerator

◄ Cockcroft-Walton generator
▼ Particle accumulator

Path of beam

Bending magnets

Beam pipe

Ring magnets

Deflector

Experimental hall

Accelerating cavity

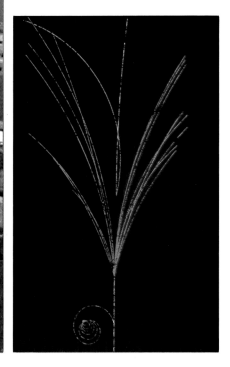

▼ Color-coded particle tracks in a bubble chamber, showing the result of a collision between a moving proton (yellow) and a stationary one. The main subatomic particles produced are pions, both positive (red) and negative (blue).

▲ How a fixed-target synchrotron operates. Particles are given their first energy boost in a Cockcroft-Walton generator, and then a linear accelerator injects them into the synchrotron. This is encased by magnets to bend the particle stream, which is given energy each lap. It is finally deflected into an experimental hall, where it collides with other particles.

The energy generated in colliding-beam machines can be colossal. It is expressed in terms of electron-volts (eV), the energy of an electron when it is accelerated by an electric field of one volt. In the Tevatron, for example, colliding particles generate energies of up to 2,000,000,000,000 electron-volts. This is enough to study evidence of the ultimate subatomic particles, quarks, from which many other particles appear to be made up.

The earliest kind of accelerators, developed in the early 1930s, included the Van de Graaf and the Cockcroft-Walton generators. The Van de Graaf machine produced the high voltages needed to accelerate particles by building up electrostatic charges. The Cockcroft-Walton machine built up voltages using alternating-voltage electricity. It is still used in modern accelerator facilities for energizing particles before they are injected into the main machine.

Part Two

Toward tomorrow

During the two to three million years we human beings or our direct ancestors have existed on Earth, we have become the dominant species. But our very success in shaping the planet for our own benefit is now threatening to destroy what we have built. Indeed, we have put the whole living world at risk.

To combat the gathering threats to our environment and way of life, such as global warming, pollution, overpopulation, and dwindling resources, we are going to need the expertise and inventiveness of the scientist and engineer as never before. But "necessity is the mother of invention": we are going to find solutions to our problems, because we must in order to survive.

Our inventiveness will also keep us blazing new trails, and seeking and conquering new frontiers. One day perhaps we will conquer that last great frontier, space, and journey to the stars.

◄ A computer-generated image of the molecular structure of an enzyme called thermolysin. The molecular modeling of organic substances by computer has become a powerful tool in biomedical research.

Future Earth

Spot facts

- The concentration of carbon dioxide in the atmosphere has risen from about 290 ppm (parts per million) a century ago to over 350 ppm today, an increase of 20 percent.

- If the build-up of carbon dioxide and other greenhouse gases continues, world temperatures could increase by as much as 4°C (7°F) by the middle of the next century.

- Each of the some 1,500 million cattle in the world emits each day on average about 250 grams (8 ounces) of methane, another greenhouse gas.

- More than 10 million hectares of forests are destroyed in the world every year. This is an area the size of the state of Ohio.

▶ Biochemists investigate the genetic make-up of plants in experiments aimed at improving agricultural crops. By treating seeds with radiation, or more recently by genetic engineering techniques, they can create new plant varieties.

One of the most pressing problems in the years ahead is how to preserve our environment, yet at the same time preserve and even improve our way of life. Thanks to our own actions in shaping the world as we want it, that world is now under threat. For example, pollution and the destruction of forests are affecting the Earth's climate and killing its wildlife.

So we must learn how to manage our planet better, to cultivate the land with greater efficiency and with greater regard for nature. And we must conserve Earth's precious resources, because they are the only ones we have.

Gaia

In Greek mythology Gaia was the goddess of the Earth, a living being. And this is the name we use today for a concept that treats the whole Earth as a living entity. We cannot simply divide our world into two separate parts – the organic, or living, and the inorganic, or non-living. This is because in order to create the world as it is today the living and non-living parts have continually interacted.

For example, our atmosphere has not always contained the oxygen on which most life now depends. Not until about 2.5 billion years ago did organisms (ancestors of plants) evolve that gave off oxygen. This began to change the existing suffocating atmosphere, dominated by carbon dioxide. The presence of the oxygen in the atmosphere allowed the evolution of the millions of different species on Earth today. It also led to the formation of the rust-red iron oxide rocks found widely across the globe.

Later, the oceans swarmed with tiny creatures with chalky skeletons. When they died in their billions, their skeletons built up and solidified into the rocks we call chalk. These are just some examples of how the living and nonliving parts of Earth have interacted.

▲ (top) Apollo astronauts snapped this picture of the Earth rising over the Moon. Pictures like this evoked the concept of "spaceship Earth," a fragile island of life and light in the dark, hostile environment of space.

▲ (bottom) The British scientist James Lovelock put forward the Gaia concept of a living Earth in 1986. It was the British novelist William Golding who suggested the name.

49

Climate

The Earth's climate – its pattern of weather year by year – remains much the same over a short period, but it can vary over a long period. For example, 20,000 years ago the Earth was in the grip of an ice age, during which much of Europe and North America was covered with glaciers. That ice age came to an end about 10,000 years ago, and gave way to our present relatively mild climate. Geologically, however, this is considered a warm interglacial period, due to end with the coming of another ice age, perhaps in a matter of centuries.

Ice ages and other climatic changes on Earth come about naturally. They may be triggered by a number of natural phenomena, such as fluctuations in the Sun's energy output and the drifting of the continents. Such changes take place over a relatively long time scale.

Other natural changes in climate may occur more suddenly and have a shorter-term effect. When some volcanoes erupt, they throw into the air vast amounts of dust. This can remain in the atmosphere for some time, blocking solar radiation and bringing about a slight cooling of

▲ Rain-forest destruction in South America. The slash-and-burn method of clearing land for agriculture is doubly harmful. It creates carbon dioxide, and it removes the trees that help the Earth "breathe." Also, the cleared land becomes infertile after only a few years; so the farmer clears more.

the climate. The impact of rocks from outer space can cause a similar effect. If the rock is large enough, the results can be catastrophic, releasing so much dust that the Earth could remain in perpetual night for months on end. This is what may have happened 65 million years ago, when the dinosaurs and many other living species died out.

Until about 200 years ago, the presence on Earth of humankind had little effect on its climate. Then the Industrial Revolution began, and factories began pumping smoke and fumes into the atmosphere as they burned coal. In the 1900s the process has accelerated, as industry has continued to expand and gasoline- and diesel-burning vehicles have proliferated.

The result is that carbon dioxide, the heavy gas produced by burning coal and oil, is building

▲ The eruption of Mount St. Helens volcano on May 18 1980, shot huge amounts of dust 20 km (over 12 mi.) high into the atmosphere.

▶ A Nimbus weather satellite monitors the concentration of ozone in the ozone layer, producing maps like this. It now regularly spots "holes" in the layer, as here (center) in October 1989.

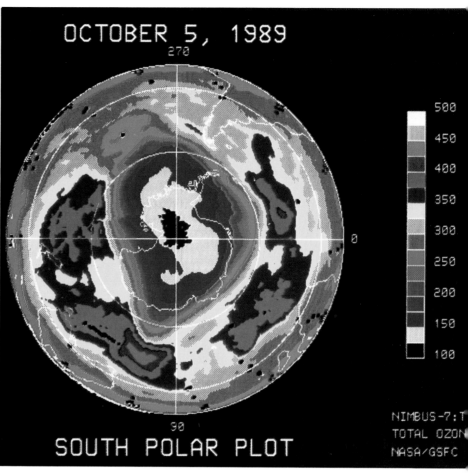

OCTOBER 5, 1989

270

90

SOUTH POLAR PLOT

500
450
400
350
300
250
200
150
100

NIMBUS-7:T
TOTAL OZON
NASA/GSFC

up in the atmosphere. Other gases are building up too. They include methane from garbage dumps and cattle, nitrogen oxides from car exhausts, and chlorofluorocarbons (CFCs) from aerosols and refrigerants. All these gases absorb heat radiation from the Earth that would otherwise escape into space.

They are turning the atmosphere into a kind of greenhouse. This "greenhouse effect" is leading to gradual global warming, which could see average world temperatures rise by up to 4°C (7°F) within 50 years. This does not seem much, but it is enough to alter our climate markedly, bringing about melting of the polar ice caps and widespread flooding worldwide.

Ozone is increasing in the lower atmosphere, but decreasing in the upper, in the ozone layer. The ozone is being broken down by chemical reactions with CFCs. If the ozone layer thins too much, more of the Sun's ultraviolet rays will get through, leading to a dramatic increase in skin cancer. They could also harm plant life.

▼ Scientists boring into the Antarctic ice to obtain an ice core. By analyzing the air in bubbles in the ice, they can estimate the temperature and composition of the atmosphere when the ice was formed.

Wildlife

Changes in climate have been one of the main influences on evolution since life began on Earth some 3.5 billion years ago. The plants and animals that were better suited to the changing climate tended to thrive, while those less suited tended to die out.

Sudden catastrophes, such as, perhaps, the impact of an asteroid 65 million years ago, brought about the extinction of hundreds of species at a stroke. But it was as a result of the mass extinction of the highly successful "terrible lizards", the dinosaurs, that the mammals were able to become dominant.

Today the human species, *Homo sapiens sapiens* (wise, wise man), shares the Earth with perhaps as many as 30 million other species, from the microscopic ameba to the massive 100-ton blue whale. But are we humans so "wise, wise"?

As a direct result of our actions in shaping the world as we want it, many species known to our ancestors have become extinct, and many more are now at risk. Those at risk include most whales, elephants, gorillas, orangutans, rhinoceroses, pandas, and koala bears. Whales, for example, are under threat from hunting, although this has been partly banned. Some whale populations, however, may be too small to survive. Gorillas and orangutans are most at risk from habitat destruction, as farmers clear

▲ A gorilla group feeding in the West African jungle under the watchful eye of the silverback, the adult male. Habitat destruction has put the species at risk.

▶ A chart that shows the march of extinction of species since 1600, and the alarming possibility that nearly 1,000 species could disappear this century.

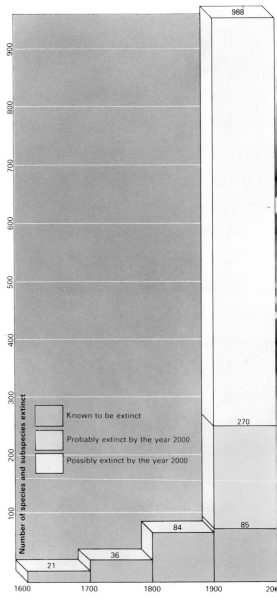

Number of species and subspecies extinct

Known to be extinct

Probably extinct by the year 2000

Possibly extinct by the year 2000

988

270

85

84

36

21

1600   1700   1800   1900   20

▲ The slaughter of whales still goes on for so-called "scientific research." But a total ban is needed to ensure their survival.

▼ A kestrel perches on a bridge. Kestrels like this man-made environment, hunting prey living on the shoulders of the road.

▲ Hunting by poachers is one of the main reasons for the decline of the African elephant. They kill for the tusks, the source of ivory.

the tropical rain forests for agriculture.

It is the wholesale destruction of these and other forests that is threatening the greatest ecological disaster. Tropical forests contain hundreds of thousands of plant and animal species, many not yet discovered. They also act as the Earth's "lungs," taking in carbon dioxide from the atmosphere in photosynthesis and giving out oxygen.

Forest trees are at risk, too, from atmospheric pollution, particularly in industrial regions. Factories and power plants burning fossil fuels release large amounts of sulfur and nitrogen oxides into the atmosphere. These pollutants combine with moisture to form droplets of acid, which fall back to Earth in the rain. The acid rain attacks trees and other plants and makes ponds and lakes unable to support life.

Other pollutants of our planet include pesticides, heavy metals and other toxic factory wastes, oil, and excess nitrates from agricultural land. They all take their toll of wildlife in one way or another, so their use must be more carefully monitored in the future.

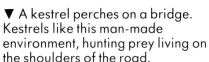

Agriculture

In the last half of this century there has been a Green Revolution in farming. This has led to an enormous increase in crop production, particularly in cereals such as wheat and rice. Greater yields have been obtained as a result of applying chemical fertilizers to the ground and pesticides to the growing crops. Better varieties of crops have been created by such techniques as irradiation and, more recently by genetic engineering.

However, the Green Revolution has passed by many of the world's poorest communities. They cannot afford the fertilizers and pesticides, but rely on traditional farming methods, which produce relatively low crop yields. One such method is slash-and-burn agriculture, in which farmers cut down and burn forest land and convert it into farmland. When the soil runs out of nutrients, they move on.

Many of the world's poor live on desert margins, where, if the seasonal rains come, they can grow crops. But when the rains fail, they are faced with starvation. The sparse vegetation of desert margins and other semi-arid land also allows people to graze livestock. But with an ever-increasing population, the land may become overgrazed so that the plants do not survive. With no plant roots to bind it, the soil gets blown away by the wind, and the land turns to desert.

Such desertification is occurring at the rate of tens of thousands of square kilometers a year, and affects as many as 100 nations. With a warming climate, the process is bound to

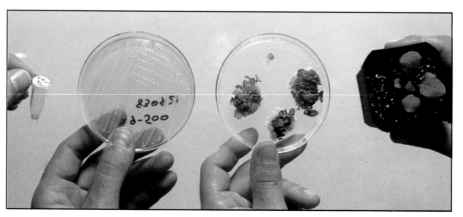

▲ Drought is a constant threat to agriculture in many parts of the world. Here in Africa, the farmers build low walls as dams to conserve water when the rains come.

◄ Steps in growing new varieties of tobacco plants by genetic engineering. The required genes are inserted, via a carrier, into soil bacteria. Plant cells become infected with the bacteria and are themselves genetically altered.

► Injecting cows with the growth hormone bovine somatotropin (BST) increases their milk yield dramatically: average yields go up by as much as 20 percent. Yet the cows do not need any more food than usual. BST can be produced in large quantities by genetically altered microorganisms in cultured animal cells. However, on most farms injecting cows on a large scale is not practical. And so genetic engineers are attempting to alter the genes in cattle embryos so that the resulting animals will overproduce the growth hormone naturally.

▼ A farmer feeding eland on a game "ranch" in Tanzania, East Africa. Raising native game animals, rather than regular cattle, makes more sense in many regions, for they are better adapted to the prevailing climatic conditions. They are farmed mainly for meat production. In other parts of Africa springbok, impalas, kudu, bontebok, and wildebeests are also farmed.

accelerate. This is bad news for world farming, which somehow has got to cope with the population explosion that is upon us.

And what an explosion it is. Every minute of every day, more than 270 babies are born into the world. And the current world population stands at more than 5 billion. It will be an estimated 8.2 billion by the year 2020. Another and more widespread Green Revolution must take place if we are to stand a chance of feeding a world population this size.

The biggest hope for increased agricultural production would seem to lie more in genetic engineering than in more and better pesticides and fertilizers. Genetic engineers are already producing new plant varieties with built-in resistance to certain diseases. Soon they should be able to produce varieties that create fertilizers, rather as beans do. This would allow farmers to use less nitrate fertilizers, which are now causing serious pollution.

Resources

Raw materials

Manufacturers use vast amounts of raw materials to make their goods. Mostly they are extracted from the ground in the form of minerals. These minerals will not last forever. Once we have used them up, it will take many millions of years for nature to replace them.

Many minerals are being mined in such quantities that they will run out in the forseeable future. Uranium, silver, gold, and platinum ores could even run out by the turn of the century. Copper and tungsten ores will not be far behind. Fortunately, the ores of our two most important construction metals, iron and aluminum, will last much longer: iron for some 300 years, aluminum for 150 years.

Strenuous efforts are being made to put off the day when the metals run out. Scientists and engineers are trying to develop new materials to replace them. These materials include composites made of synthetic resins and fibers, and

▲ A futuristic house called Xanadu, at Kissimmee, in central Florida. It is an energy-saving design built of synthetic materials. The roof domes were made by spraying polyurethane foam on large balloons.

ceramic products, which are made from minerals found plentifully in the Earth's crust.

The other conservation approach is recycling metals after use. Steel scrap is already being recycled on a large scale, as is aluminum. In the case of aluminum in particular, the saving brought about by recycling lies not so much in conserving the metal but in conserving energy. This is because the aluminum smelting process consumes large amounts of electricity.

Energy

The bulk of the world's energy at present comes from burning fossil fuels: oil, natural gas, and coal. Oil and natural gas could run out in the next century, although new fields are still being discovered. Coal will last for much longer, maybe for hundreds of years. All three fossil fuels should perhaps not be burned at all. They will have far greater value in the long term as chemical raw materials to make plastics and other synthetic products.

Various sources of energy will need to be harnessed sooner rather than later to replace the fossil fuels. The use of renewable sources, such as wind, water (hydroelectric), solar, and geothermal power will increase. But all these are limited to certain locations. Nuclear-fission power will also probably become more widespread, but its development will by dogged by problems of safety and the disposal of radioactive wastes. Ultimately, the world's energy salvation lies in the harnessing of nuclear-fusion power. This would use as fuel heavy hydrogen, which is found in almost unlimited amounts in the oceans.

▼ A collection point for waste aluminum cans in the Florida Keys. The cans are being collected for recycling. Recycling not only helps conserve raw materials, it also helps conserve energy – the energy needed to process the raw materials. Processing aluminum ore is particularly power-consuming.

▲ This particle accelerator at Sandia Laboratories in New Mexico is used in experiments on nuclear fusion. To bring about fusion, a gaseous plasma of heavy hydrogen atoms (deuterium and tritium) are heated to about 100 million °C (180 million °F). The problems are how to heat and control the plasma.

▶ A boy feeds animal dung into a generator producing methane in a village in India. The dung is mixed with water, and ferments. Methane gas is given off. The resulting waste is useful as fertilizer.

Frontiers in medicine

Spot facts

● *The dwindling forests of the world probably contain a treasure trove of drugs waiting to be discovered. The Pacific yew which grows on the West Coast, has recently yielded a drug called taxol, which has proved effective against some cancers.*

● *By injecting themselves with human growth hormone, people over the age of 60 can look and feel 20 years younger.*

● *Japanese scientists are developing a "smart pill" the size of a peanut which contains a microcomputer and sensors. It will measure temperature and the concentration of chemicals as it passes through the body and transmit the results to a computer screen.*

▶ A microbiologist investigating an unknown micro-organism that causes disease. He is heavily protected to prevent accidental contamination by t he organism, which could be transmitted by contact or through the air by breathing.

The twentieth century has seen spectacular success in the diagnosis and treatment of disease, and breakthroughs in medicine are still coming thick and fast. The widespread use of antibiotics and mass immunization continue to save millions of people from once-deadly diseases. New machines are continually being developed to help diagnosis. In surgery, organ transplants have become routine; so has microsurgery to repair delicate nerves and tissues. A revolution is being brought about by genetic engineering, which could in the years ahead help eliminate hereditary defects.

Beating disease

In Roman times, some 2,000 years ago, people were lucky to live beyond their twenties. Even in 1950, the average life expectancy in the world was less than 50 years. But today Japanese women can on average look forward to reaching their 81st birthday. Their menfolk, however, on average live only about 75 years.

People in developed countries like Japan have a high life expectancy today, partly because of better nutrition, but mainly because of better medical care. Modern medical practice can prevent, successfully treat, and even eliminate diseases that were once deadly.

It is a different story, however, in developing, or Third World, countries in Africa, South America, and Southeast Asia. There life expectancy is still low. One of the biggest killers is malnutrition and associated problems, particularly diarrhea. This complaint is estimated to kill, or contribute to the deaths of, at least 25 million children each year.

For those with access to it, modern medicine has a formidable array of weaponry available to combat disease. Diseases are caused by a multitude of microorganisms. Bacteria cause diseases such as typhoid, diphtheria, and whooping cough. Viruses cause influenza, measles, and AIDS. The best-known parasite disease is malaria.

All these diseases can be killers. These days most of them, or the effects they produce, can be treated with drugs. These may be chemicals, such as sulfa drugs; or antibiotics, which are produced by certain microorganisms, such as the fungus *Penicillium*. With the help of computers, researchers are now finding ways of making "designer drugs," specially tailored to link up with the molecules of invading germs.

Modern medicine is also concerned with disease prevention via immunization. Patients are inoculated with vaccines, or given them orally. Vaccines are generally weakened or killed germs, which stimulate the body's defenses to produce specific antibodies against them. So if the patient is later exposed to those germs, the antibodies can deal with them.

A worldwide mass-vaccination program against smallpox eliminated the disease from the face of the Earth by 1980. A similar program against diseases such as diphtheria, measles, tetanus, whooping cough, and polio, could save millions of children every year.

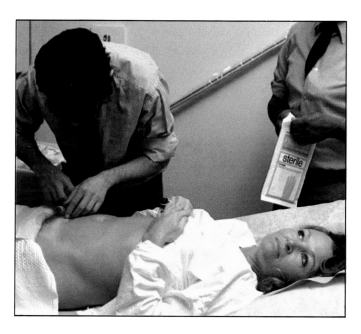

▲ Extracting some of the fluid surrounding the developing fetus in a pregnant woman. Analysis of the fluid may reveal genetic defects in the fetus. Screening patients to get advance warning of disease now plays an important role in medicine.

▲ Immunizing children in El Salvador. In a campaign in the 1980s, 400,000 people were immunized there in one day against measles, whooping cough, diphtheria, and tetanus. Such campaigns hold the key to preventive medicine.

Diagnosis

For many diseases there are as yet no preventive measures like immunization. They include AIDS, diabetes, cervical cancer in women, Down's syndrome, and hemophilia. The root cause of each of these diseases is different.

AIDS is caused by a virus. Diabetes can occur as a result of the malfunction of a body organ (the pancreas); cervical cancer is the abnormal growth of cells in the cervix. Down's syndrome results from a faulty chromosome; hemophilia, from a faulty gene on a chromosome.

Various techniques are adopted to detect the presence of such diseases, which may allow early treatment and in some cases a cure. A simple blood test can indicate diabetes. Treating the blood with an enzyme will reveal if the level of glucose is abnormal. A "smear" from the cervix will reveal under the microscope if cancerous or precancerous cells are present.

Many diseases can be diagnosed by using antibodies as "homing" devices to link up with the disease-carrying microorganisms. The

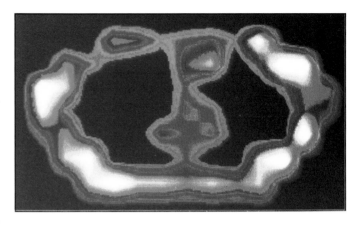

▲▼ An MRI scanner produces an image of a cross section of a patient's body (above). The patient lies inside a cylinder in a strong magnetic field and is exposed to a "dose" of radio waves (below). Atoms in the body absorb the radiation, and afterward give it out again as radio signals. A computer analyzes the signals and can form an image of the internal tissues.

Magnet coils   Radio-frequency coils

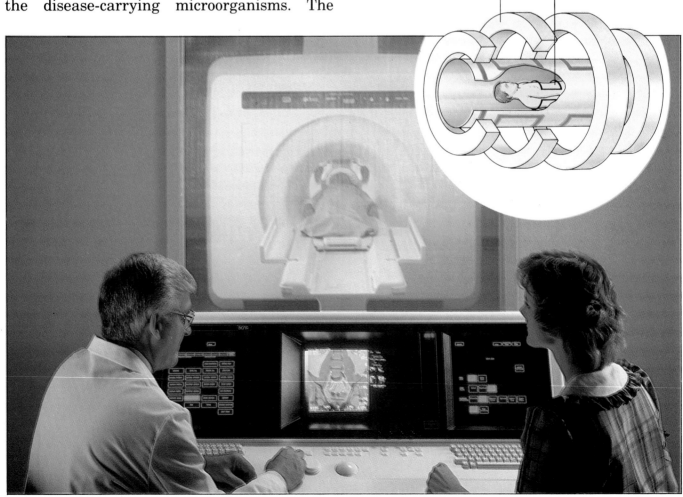

linked antibodies can be detected by means of a fluorescent or radioactive "label."

As far as genetic defects are concerned, techniques are now available that can test for them in the fetus developing in a mother's womb. In a technique called amniocentesis, some of the amniotic fluid around the fetus is withdrawn. It contains cells from the fetus, which can be examined for genetic defects.

To help them find the best place to withdraw the fluid, doctors use an ultrasonic scanner. This is a machine that produces images by bouncing waves of ultrasound off internal structures, like a sound radar. Unlike X-rays, sound waves do not harm the fetus. This machine is one of several types of scanner used to check a patient's condition and provide early warning of disease or abnormality in the body.

CAT (computerized axial tomography) scanning using X-rays enables doctors to see body tissues and structures which ordinary X-ray radiography cannot. In the CAT scanner a patient is exposed to a thin, fan-shaped beam of X-rays. The intensity of the rays passing through a "slice" of the body is measured by an array of detectors. The X-ray source is moved around the patient, a few degrees at a time, and the measurements are fed to a computer. The computer then builds up a detailed image of the tissues in the body slice scanned.

Another scanning technique, called MRI (magnetic resonance imaging), creates images by passing radio waves through the body in a strong magnetic field.

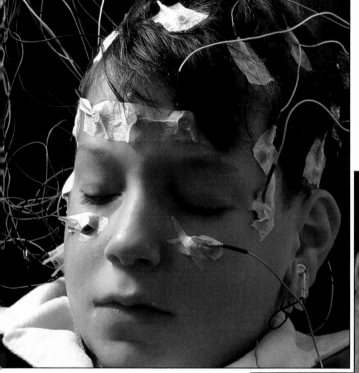

▲ A boy wired up for EEG, or electroencephalography. EEG records the electrical activity of the brain through about 16 electrodes stuck to the face and scalp. The electrical brain waves are fed to a machine which makes a permanent record of them by pen. EEGs can reveal much about brain disorders.

▶ A scintigram of the spine shows the presence of a cancerous tumor (white). It was produced by injecting a radioactive substance into the body and then taking a photograph with a gamma-ray camera.

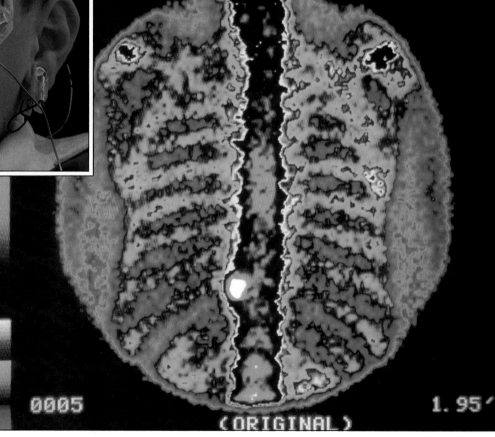

Mending the body

When serious disease or injury strikes the body, it is often the surgeon who is called in to repair the damage. These days surgeons can perform operations that would have been considered miracles only a few decades ago. They can transplant organs from one person to another, and replace body parts with metal and synthetic prostheses. They can give blood transfusions to unborn babies inside the womb, and also perform major operations on them there. Working under a microscope, doctors can connect nerves as thin as a human hair.

In an extraordinary series of operations in 1990, French surgeons attached a man's severed foot to his arm. It remained there for seven months while they repaired his damaged leg. Then they put it back in its rightful place.

Perhaps the most dramatic examples of the surgeon's art are the organ transplants. The heart, lung, liver, and kidney can now be successfully transplanted if a suitable donor is available. The surgery itself is not that difficult – a heart transplant may take only four hours. The main problem is the rejection of the new organ by the body's immune system. After all, its job is to fight and reject foreign substances.

So transplant patients must take immuno-suppressive drugs for the rest of their life to prevent rejection. Some patients experience unpleasant side effects with existing drugs, such as cyclosporin. But trials with a new Japanese "wonder drug," FK 506, indicate that it is more effective against rejection, has few side effects, and does not immobilize the body's immune system.

There is, however, a lack of donor organs. In the United States alone some 1,500 people are on waiting lists for a heart or heart-lung transplant at any one time. Their best hope of survival lies perhaps in an artificial heart,

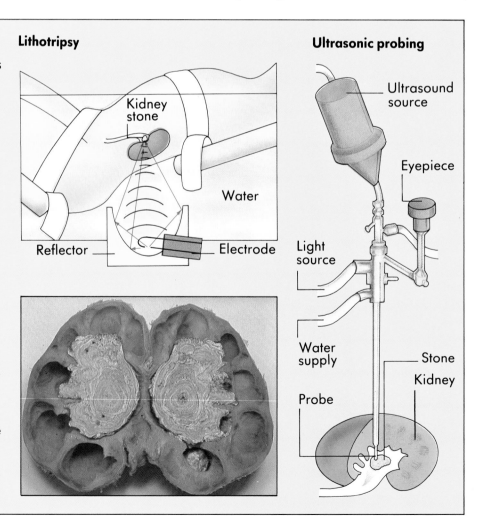

Sound destruction

A painful disease of the kidneys is kidney stones. Mineral growths called stones sometimes build up inside the urine-gathering space in the kidneys (bottom picture right). Until recently surgery was usually the only method of removing them. But two recent methods avoid surgery, using instead sound waves to break up the stones.

In a technique called lithotripsy the patient is placed in a water bath. High-energy sound waves are then channeled on to the stones and break them up. The fragments leave in the urine.

In the other method a special probe is inserted into the kidney itself. This enables the surgeon to see the stones and destroy them with ultrasonic waves. Afterwards water is channeled through the probe to flush away the stone fragments.

Such treatments are some of the methods being used to avoid major surgery, which is stressful on the patient and requires a lengthy recuperation time.

Lithotripsy

Kidney stone

Water

Reflector

Electrode

Ultrasonic probing

Ultrasound source

Eyepiece

Light source

Water supply

Probe

Stone

Kidney

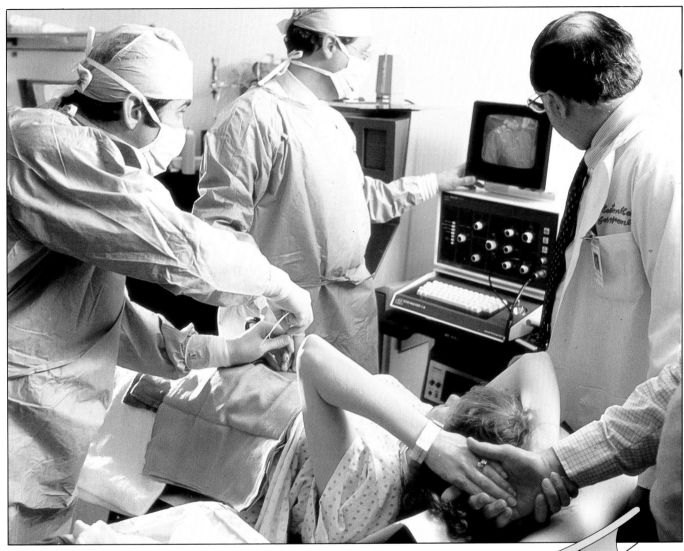

▲ Surgeons give a blood transfusion to a fetus inside the mother's womb. This is done when a mother with Rh-negative blood carries an Rh-positive foetus. Most people are Rh-positive.

▶ A modern technique for unblocking arteries uses a balloon catheter. This instrument penetrates the deposits and then breaks them up.

which could be used until a donor is found.

The original artificial heart, the Jarvik-7, first used in a human being in the early 1980s, required bulky equipment to keep it pumping. New designs now undergoing clinical trials are much more compact and are battery powered, giving the patient mobility. They are implanted in the body next to the patient's own heart, assisting it rather than replacing it.

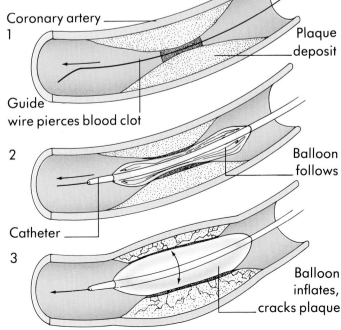

Coronary artery

1

Plaque deposit

Guide wire pierces blood clot

2

Balloon follows

Catheter

3

Balloon inflates, cracks plaque

Genetic engineering

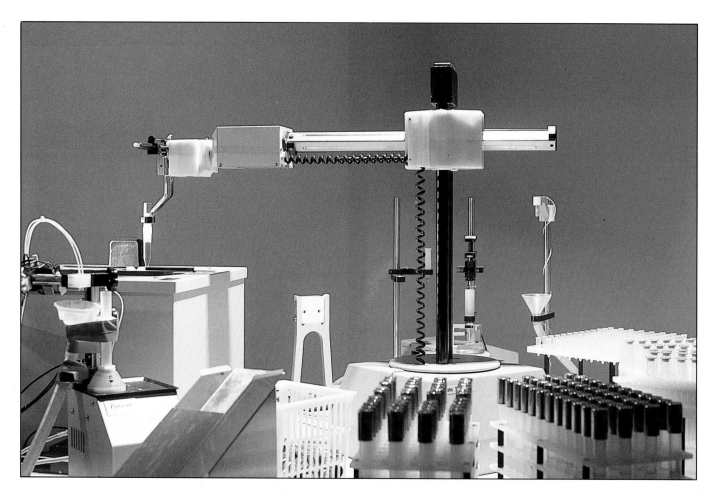

As many as 3,000 human diseases are caused by defects in the genes. These are the units of inheritance, which are passed from generation to generation. Cystic fibrosis, spina bifida, muscular dystrophy, hemophilia, and sickle-cell anemia are examples of genetic disorders. But there is now hope that in the coming years such diseases will be eliminated by identifying and altering the genes responsible.

The process of manipulating genes is known as genetic engineering. It has become one of the main branches of biotechnology. Genetic engineers have made remarkable progress in recent years. In agriculture, for example, they have created crops that are resistant to herbicides, or weed killers. They transferred genes from a herbicide-resistant species into the crop plants, which then also became resistant.

Genetic engineers have made a growth hormone for cattle, called BST, which increases milk yield. They have also produced in a similar way the human hormone insulin.

Deoxyribonucleic acid (DNA)

DNA has a "double helix" structure, with two chains of sugar and phosphate groups twisted around each other. Each chain has side units called bases, which link like the rungs of a ladder. DNA reproduces, or replicates itself, by splitting down the middle, whereupon new base, sugar, and phosphate units join each strand to create identical "daughter" DNA helices.

Daughter DNA

Bases

Parent DNA

New chains

Phosphate and sugar chains

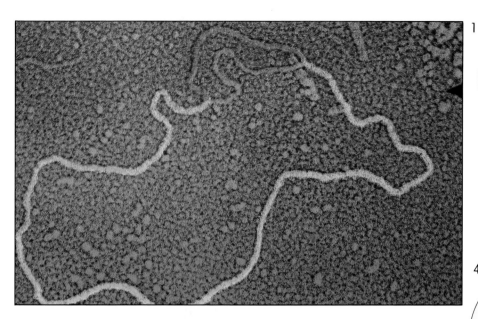

◀▲ Robots (left) help scientists manipulate DNA, and map its genes. Mapping can be done (above) using genetic "probes" (red), which stick to particular genes (blue).

▼ (left) *E. coli* bacteria used to make insulin for treating diabetes. This diabetic (below) works in a biotechnology unit that produces insulin in this way.

Cloning genes

▲ The first stage in cloning is to add a restriction enzyme to DNA containing the desired gene (1). This cuts the DNA (2) and releases the fragment carrying the gene (blue). A small circle of DNA called a plasmid (5) is also cut by the enzyme (4). The DNA fragment enters the plasmid and the ends link up. The genetically altered plasmid (3) is now ready to enter a host cell.

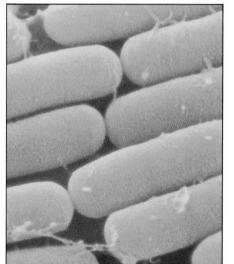

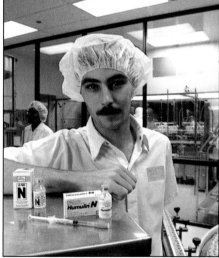

Both hormones are produced by gene-splicing. The gene responsible for producing the hormone is inserted into a bacterium. The genetically altered bacterium reproduces and forms replicas, or clones, of itself with the new genetic makeup. And in each new cell, the genes order the production of the hormone.

Genetic engineering deals with the "brains" behind the living cell, a spiral molecule called DNA (deoxyribonucleic acid). DNA, which resides in the nucleus, carries the genes that direct every function of, and impart every characteristic to, the living organism.

In gene-cloning experiments, certain enzymes, called restriction enzymes, are used to cut out the part of the DNA that carries the desired gene. This part is then combined with a so-called vector, or carrier, such as a plasmid (a small circle of bacterial DNA) or a virus. This transports it into the nucleus of the host cell.

Information technology

The rapid handling, processing, and transmission of information of all kinds are of ever-increasing importance in the modern world. They are critical in such diverse fields as space travel, weather forecasting, and air-traffic control. International businesses and stock markets could not function without them; nor could chemical factories, oil refineries, or modern newspapers. Computers are at the forefront of this information revolution, able to process information at lightning speed. Now relying on microchip technology, they are cheap enough to be available to almost everybody.

Electronic brainpower

Every day of our lives we constantly give out and receive information in one form or another. The input of information about the world around us comes from our senses, particularly sight and hearing. Our eyes, ears, and other senses register the incoming information and send signals to the brain. The brain processes and maybe acts on the information signals it receives, drawing on other information stored in its memory. The processed information is also stored. It may be communicated, or output, to others via speech or writing.

Broadly speaking, computers work in much the same way as the brain, and are often called electronic brains. They have devices to input data, as computer information is called. They process this data, using instructions and other data stored in their memory. The processed data may then be stored or output.

In the brain the memory takes the form of millions of nerve cells. The storage of information in the cells is probably electrochemical: the electric impulses representing information trigger slight changes in brain chemicals. Computers also handle data in the form of electrical impulses. Their memory consists of tiny "cells," or rather miniature electronic circuits, etched on wafers, or chips, of silicon. They store data as different electrical states, representing the zeros and ones in the digital code used by computers.

For all its similarities with the human brain, a computer cannot think for itself. It can only do what it is told, or programmed, to do. It can, however, be programmed to learn by experience as humans do. This is one aspect of what is called artificial intelligence, the intelligence of computers.

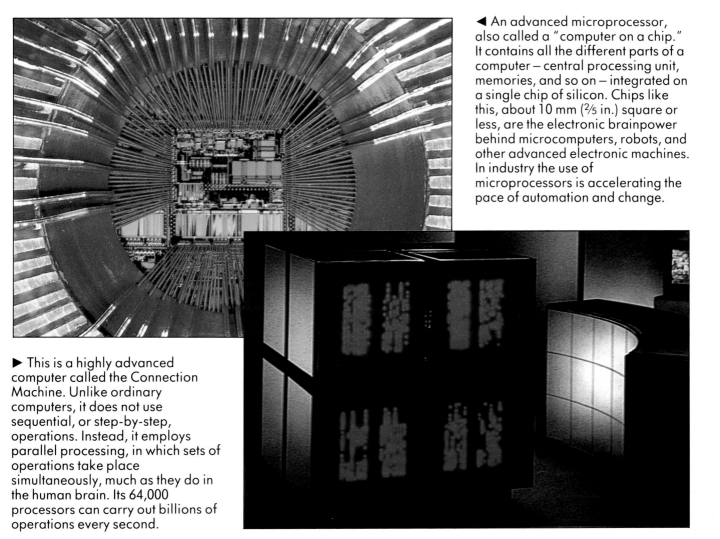

◀ An advanced microprocessor, also called a "computer on a chip." It contains all the different parts of a computer – central processing unit, memories, and so on – integrated on a single chip of silicon. Chips like this, about 10 mm (²⁄₅ in.) square or less, are the electronic brainpower behind microcomputers, robots, and other advanced electronic machines. In industry the use of microprocessors is accelerating the pace of automation and change.

▶ This is a highly advanced computer called the Connection Machine. Unlike ordinary computers, it does not use sequential, or step-by-step, operations. Instead, it employs parallel processing, in which sets of operations take place simultaneously, much as they do in the human brain. Its 64,000 processors can carry out billions of operations every second.

Speedier computing

The modern computer based on silicon microchips is already an amazing machine. And increasingly novel methods are being developed to input information into it to make it more versatile. Yet researchers are still forging ahead to make it an even more powerful tool in science, business, industry, and everyday life.

For example, they are seeking to increase the speed of the most powerful supercomputers, such as the Cray. The speed of computers is expressed in terms of "flops," an acronym of "floating-point operations per second." Already, some supercomputers have a speed measured in giga-flops, or billions of flops. Tomorrow's supercomputers will be a thousand times faster, with a speed measured in teraflops. Teraflop performance will require the use of masses of processors computing in parallel, rather like the brain does. For this reason they are termed massively parallel computers.

Such computers should be on the market early next century. But by that time the silicon chip might be on the way out, and "molecular" chips might be taking over. These are chips based upon organic molecules. One familiar example of a molecule used in electronics is the liquid crystal, used for displays in watches. Such displays (LCDs) work because the liquid

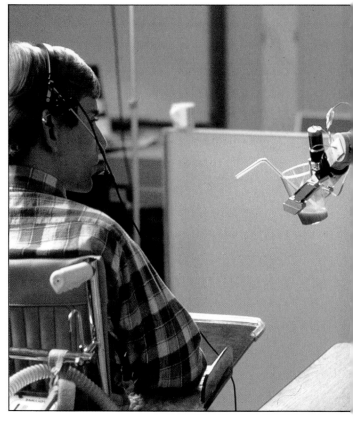

▲ A computer-controlled robot offers a drink to its physically disabled operator. Computers are proving a boon to the disabled, who can instruct them, via sensors, by movements of any kind.

crystal alters when electricity is applied to it. Other molecules may also be made to change their electrical state, or manipulate electric current, rather like a silicon chip does. But molecules are much smaller than silicon chips.

It is probable that complex organic molecules such as proteins will prove suitable. Since they will be similar to the proteins found in living things, molecular chips are often called biochips. Almost certainly, the biochip proteins will be tailor-made to perform certain functions. Chip designers will use computer-based molecular-modeling techniques. Perhaps, in the long term, it will prove possible to mass-produce the proteins by genetic-engineering techniques.

◄ A blind student works at a computer terminal. Using his fingertips, he reads a printout in braille of text he has written. Via the braille printer and a modem, he can also receive other information.

▲ An air-traffic controller using a terminal with a voice-recognition facility. Voice recognition by computers is an expanding field.

▼ A shopper uses a fingerprint to verify her identity when paying by check. A computer compares it with prints it has in its memory.

Expanding databases

Thanks to their ever-increasing memory capacity, computers are able to cope with the information explosion that is upon us. The explosion is particularly apparent in scientific and technical literature, with articles and papers appearing in print at the rate of up to two million a year.

Scientists conducting research need to have knowledge of, and refer to, experiments and papers in their own and related fields, nationwide and worldwide. To locate and retrieve selected information from millions of articles, past and present, would be a daunting and time-consuming task without the speed and expertise of a computer.

Individual scientists, or even universities, could not hope to keep up-to-date records in their computers. So what they do is link up with specialist companies which have compiled and stored the information in a so-called database. The scientist, for a fee, can then access the database through a personal computer (PC), a modem, and the telephone network.

Many of the first databases were, indeed, set up to keep track of scientific literature. But many additional kinds of databases are now available: drugs for doctors, legal information and case histories for lawyers, financial and commercial information for business people and industrialists, and so on. Organizations also operate databases for more limited circulation: for example, the police, banks, and local government.

Databases covering subjects of more general interest are available to the general public through terminals at many public libraries or, for a person with a computer and modem, by subscribing to a service offering access to databases. Information from the databases is accessed via the telephone network and displayed on the computer screen.

One of the latest developments in database technology is the CD-ROM (compact disk, read only memory). This is a compact disk that stores information in the same way that an ordinary compact disk stores music: as a series of microscopic pits in the surface. The disk is played back on a disk drive and read by laser, and the information is displayed on a screen.

A single CD-ROM disk has a capacity of over 500 megabytes: the equivalent of 100,000 pages of printed text, or the data on over 500 one-megabyte floppy disks. CD-ROM databases are already available covering a wide range of topics, including the Bible, Shakespeare, world atlases, dictionaries, and encyclopedias.

▼ The computer control room of the Chase Manhattan Bank in New York City. Each major bank has a huge database, comprising the detailed accounts of millions of private and business customers. It is also linked with other banks.

▼ A computerized tax center, which holds records of millions of people and businesses. The ease with which this and other privileged and personal information can be stored and accessed is a worrying feature of the Computer Age.

▶ A policemen on patrol taps into the central police computer from the portable terminal in his patrol car to run a check on a suspicious vehicle and its driver. The police computer database carries vast amounts of information, such as the habits and haunts of known criminals and their associates, their MO (*modus operandi*, method of working), solved and unsolved crimes, and stolen goods and vehicles.

▼ The control room of the British Civil Aviation Authority centers on a powerful computer. It ties in with air-traffic control centers around the country to monitor airliner movements along the air routes, the highways of the air. Most aspects of aviation are now computerized, and the latest aircraft, such as the Airbus A320, operate via a fly-by-wire system masterminded by computers.

Transportation trends

Improvements in engineering technology in the coming years will continue to increase the speed, comfort, and reliability of transportation by sea, land, and air. But such improvements will have to be married to increased levels of safety and fuel economy. They will also have to be more friendly to the environment to reduce the amount of pollution in the atmosphere.

The high-tech answer would appear to lie in novel designs and computer-controlled systems. But the low technology of yesteryear could also return in the form of sailing ships and airships, for example.

At sea

Surface-skimming hydrofoils and hovercraft have spearheaded a dramatic increase in the speed of water transportation in recent years. They have now been joined by large oceangoing catamarans, such as the SeaCats, which ride mainly on twin side hulls, with the main hull largely out of the water.

The diesel engine is still the main power source for ships, with steam turbines being used for some large vessels. These include giant aircraft carriers like the USS *Nimitz*. Unlike ordinary ships, which use oil as fuel, the *Nimitz* is nuclear-powered. So are most missile-carrying submarines.

Nuclear vessels have a reactor to generate heat, which is used to boil water into steam to drive steam turbines. At present only a few civilian vessels, such as the NS *Savannah* and the German *Otto Hahn*, have been nuclear-powered, and they have proved uneconomic.

▲ The SeaCat *Hoverspeed Great Britain*. In June 1990 it crossed the Atlantic in 80 hours and reclaimed for Great Britain the Blue Riband title for the fastest Atlantic crossing.

▼ The Japanese tanker *Shinaitoku Maru*, launched in 1980, is fitted with computer-controlled sails as well as diesel engines. Sail-assistance on ships helps save fuel.

On land

On the roads

The success of the automobile, born over a century ago, is beginning to create all kinds of problems, which will increase as the years go by. For one thing the street and highway networks in many countries can no longer cope with the increasing volume of motor traffic.

Motor traffic is not only strangling the cities, it is also poisoning them with exhaust fumes containing lead and toxic gases such as carbon monoxide. A reduction of lead in the environment is being brought about by the increasing use of lead-free gasoline. There are two main approaches to reducing other exhaust pollutants. One is to fit a catalytic converter in the vehicle exhaust system, which converts poisonous fumes into harmless ones. The other is to use engines which burn fuel with more air and with greater efficiency.

Precise engine tuning also helps reduce undesirable exhaust emissions. Increasingly, cars will use on-board microcomputers to keep the engine well-tuned and control other systems for optimum performance. The widespread use of electric cars would solve most pollution problems, but the practical electric car is still a long way off.

On the rails

A switch from the personal transportation of the car to the public transportation of the train would provide another solution to traffic congestion and pollution on the highway. Trains, with a centralized power source and large capacity, are well suited to the efficient mass transportation of passengers and goods. Routes are in operation that offer intercity travel at speeds up to 290 km/h: this figure is achieved by the French TGV ("Train à Grande Vitesse"). Speeds of up to 500 km/h (over 300 mph) are in prospect when various maglev (magnetically levitated) projects get under way.

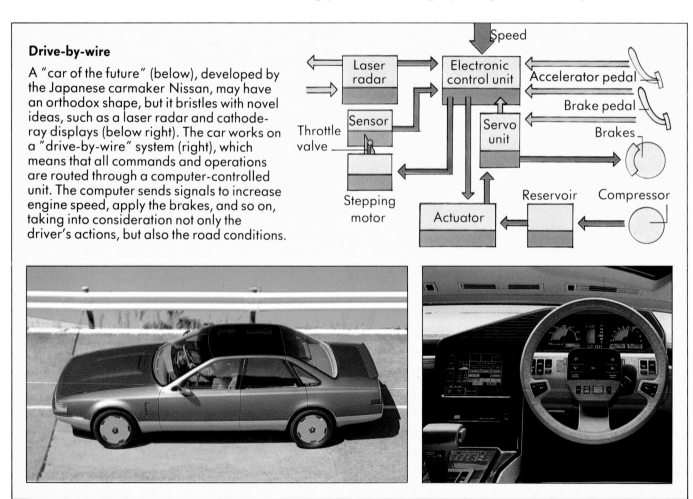

Drive-by-wire

A "car of the future" (below), developed by the Japanese carmaker Nissan, may have an orthodox shape, but it bristles with novel ideas, such as a laser radar and cathode-ray displays (below right). The car works on a "drive-by-wire" system (right), which means that all commands and operations are routed through a computer-controlled unit. The computer sends signals to increase engine speed, apply the brakes, and so on, taking into consideration not only the driver's actions, but also the road conditions.

◄ A Japanese maglev (magnetically levitated) test vehicle, which is suspended above the track it runs on by magnetic forces. It is the prototype for the next generation of high-speed trains. It carries a powerful on-board magnet, which sets up an electric current in coils embedded in the track. The current in these coils in turn sets up a magnetic field that repels the field of the on-board magnet, with the result that the vehicle rises above the track.

▼ The Pendolino, an Italian design for a tilt-train, one that leans over when it goes around corners. This design enables the train to travel at higher speeds than usual on existing curved track without throwing the passengers off-balance. High-speed trains like the TGV have to run on specially built straight track.

In the air

◄ The instrument panel in the cockpit of the Airbus A320 airliner. The plane operates on a fly-by-wire system, in which the movements of the pilot's control stick are channeled to the control surfaces not by mechanical linkages, but by means of electrical signals along wires.

▼ (left) A key to the instrument panel of the Airbus A320: (1) the control stick; (2), (3) and (4) cathode-ray tube displays, showing simulated flight and navigation instruments, and engineering systems data; (5) the flight control unit.

▼ (right) The electronic flight control system (EFCS) of the A320 controls the plane's path and attitude, acting on movement of the stick control.

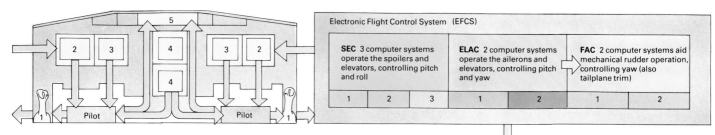

Electronic Flight Control System (EFCS)

SEC 3 computer systems operate the spoilers and elevators, controlling pitch and roll			ELAC 2 computer systems operate the ailerons and elevators, controlling pitch and yaw		FAC 2 computer systems aid mechanical rudder operation, controlling yaw (also tailplane trim)	
1	2	3	1	2	1	2

It is in the air that the most exciting developments in transportation are taking place. Conventional aircraft are constantly being improved to make them safer and more fuel-efficient. The new generation of airliners, such as the European Airbus A320, are equipped with fly-by-wire controls. These use electrical signals to connect the pilot's control stick with the plane's control surfaces.

In the interests of fuel economy, engines such as the propfan are being developed. The propfan has a multibladed propeller like a fan, which can operate efficiently at high air speeds, unlike ordinary propellers.

Many novel-looking aircraft are also appearing in the skies. They include the forward-swept-wing design and the scissor-wing. The scissor-wing craft has a wing that swivels on top of the fuselage for cruising flight: one half sweeps forward, the other backward.

Another design is the X-wing. The X-wing

▼ The numerous computer systems of the EFCS send signals to hydraulic actuators, which move the control surfaces: the ailerons, spoilers, elevators, and rudder. They respond to the pilot's movements of the control stick, taking into consideration the perfect flight behavior data stored in their memory banks.

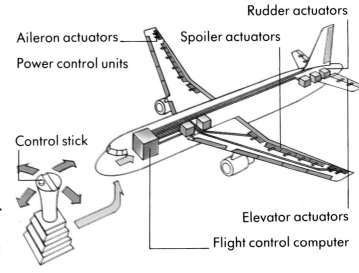

Rudder actuators
Aileron actuators
Spoiler actuators
Power control units
Control stick
Elevator actuators
Flight control computer

▲ A propfan engine mounted on a Gulfstream 2 business jet for test flights. This cross between a turboprop and a turbofan jet engine was developed by NASA. The fanlike blade design enables it to improve greatly on the performance of the ordinary turboprop and to offer much greater economy than a conventional turbofan.

◄ The novel X-29 research plane practices a simulated refueling with a KC-135 aircraft in 1988. It was the 200th flight of this plane with a forward-swept wing, which creates less drag at high speeds than a swept-back wing. The X-29 is another NASA project, managed by the Ames-Dryden Flight Research Facility in California.

craft takes off vertically with the X-shaped wing spinning like a helicopter rotor. For forward flight, the rotor is stopped and thereafter acts as an ordinary fixed wing. The idea of this design is to produce a vertical take off and landing (VTOL) machine that can fly as fast forward as a conventional fixed-wing plane. Another design for a VTOL machine, the tilt-rotor craft, is already at an advanced stage. A prototype craft, called the V-22 Osprey, made its first successful flight in April 1989.

Designs for spaceplanes, able to travel into space and back, are also on the drawing board.

The idea is that they will have a new kind of jet/rocket engine that will be able to breathe air while traveling through the atmosphere. This would avoid having to use on-board liquid oxygen, which is heavy, when there is already oxygen outside in the atmosphere. The engine will switch to a small on-board supply of liquid oxygen for injection into orbit.

Such a plane could be used as a satellite launcher, or as a high-speed transport to whisk people on long-distance journeys around the world. Mostly they would travel above the atmosphere at 25 times the speed of sound.

Space frontiers

Spot facts

● It would take at least 30 flights of the space shuttle to ferry the materials into orbit to construct the proposed U.S. space station Freedom.

● Construction materials to build human habitats in deep space will be obtained by mining on the Moon.

● A radio message was beamed into the heavens from Earth via the Arecibo radio telescope in Puerto Rico in 1974. It carried scientific information about our planet and its inhabitants in an ingenious digital and pictorial code. By now it should have reached several star systems with planets like our own.

● Mini H-bombs might be a way of propelling spacecraft at the very high speeds needed to make interstellar travel possible in the future.

Space is regarded as the last great frontier of humankind. Human beings, having established a firm foothold in space, will continue to push back the frontier with increasing confidence. By the end of this century, an American space station will probably have joined the Soviet Union's *Mir* in orbit. Preparations will have been made for a return to the Moon, and detailed plans advanced for manned missions to the Red Planet, Mars. Maybe by then we will have received messages from intelligent beings on other worlds in space and know for sure that we are not alone in the Universe.

▶ A fanciful view of an orbiting space station, built like a modern city business center. In reality, space stations will not feature high-rise blocks like this, but interconnected cylindrical modules.

Other worlds

Earth is a tiny speck in the Universe: a small planet circling around an average star (the Sun) in an average galaxy (the Milky Way). In the Universe as a whole there are many billions of galaxies. Huge numbers of them contain many millions of stars like the Sun and presumably many millions of planets like the Earth. On some of these planets it is highly likely that life has evolved, as it has on Earth.

The increasing awareness that there must be other intelligent life somewhere in space led in 1960 to the first program in the search for extraterrestrial intelligence, or SETI. It was carried out by the U.S. astronomer Frank Drake under the title of Project Ozma, named after the princess in *The Wizard of Oz*. He scanned the heavens with a radio telescope at Green Bank in West Virginia, searching for extraordinary radio signals that would indicate transmission by an intelligent life-form.

Drake's search was fruitless, but it led to many other similar projects, which in 30 years devoted more than 200,000 hours to SETI. They have targeted hundreds of stars like the Sun that could have Earth-like planets. But as yet no "intelligent" signals have been received.

Astronomers tune into the heavens on different wavelengths, particularly 21 cm. This is the wavelength of radio waves emitted by atoms of hydrogen, the most abundant element in the Universe. This would seem to be a natural choice for interstellar communications.

▶ Beta Pictoris is a star in the southern heavens that has a disk of rock and dust around it. We see the disc edge-on in this false-color picture. Planets may have already formed in the disk.

▼ The 26-m (85-ft.) radio telescope at Harvard Massachusetts, which has been "listening" for intelligent signals from space since 1983.

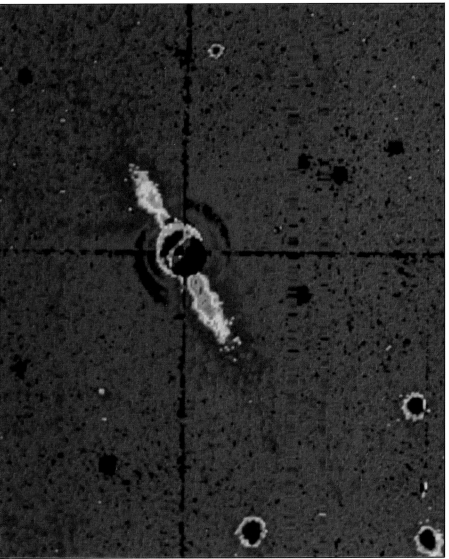

Space station *Freedom*

The Soviet Union launched the first experimental space station, *Salyut 1*, into orbit in 1971. It was designed to support a human crew for weeks or months at a time. It was not in itself successful, but it paved the way for a series of highly successful craft of similar design, notably *Salyut 6* (launched 1977) and *Salyut 7* (1982). The Salyuts, in turn, paved the way for the latest Soviet design, *Mir*.

In the United States NASA launched the first U.S. space station, *Skylab*, in 1973. This was outstandingly successful over a nine-month period, during which time it was visited by three teams of three astronauts. The last team stayed for a record 84 days, demonstrating for the first time that, properly protected, human beings could make their home in space.

NASA's long-term plans for a permanent space station to replace *Skylab* were shelved when most of its resources were switched in the 1970s to getting the space shuttle operational. But in 1984, President Ronald Reagan gave the go-ahead for a space station, which was later named *Freedom*. Europe, Canada, and Japan also joined in to give the project an international flavor.

Freedom was conceived in a modular design. Four interconnected cylindrical modules would be attached to a beam more than 150 m (500 ft.) long, which would also carry large panels of solar cells for electricity generation. The whole station would be carried into space piecemeal by the space shuttle, and put together in orbit about 300 km (almost 200 mi.) above the Earth.

NASA was to be responsible for the overall assembly of the space station and for the provision of two of the main modules. One is the habitation module, to provide accommodation for an international crew of eight, and the other is the U.S. laboratory module. These modules would measure about 15 m (50 ft.) long and 4.5 m (15 ft.) in diameter. At this size they can be fitted into the shuttle orbiter's payload bay.

Europe, through the European Space Agency

▶ (top) It is the turn of the century, and a space shuttle is inching its way in to dock with the newly completed space station *Freedom*. The four main modules of the station are located in the middle of the long trussed beam structure. Those on the right are the two U.S. modules, which are connected by so-called resources nodes. These have docking ports for visiting craft. On the opposite side of the beam are the other two main modules, the European and the Japanese.

▶ (bottom) The eight-member crew of *Freedom* would be able to enjoy a regular shower, a luxury denied to most astronauts. Here a prototype shower is being tested under the brief weightlessness possible in an arcing aircraft.

◀ In November 1985 on shuttle mission 61-B Jerry Ross practices erecting beam structures similar to those that would be needed to build the space station. Machines called beam builders, capable of fabricating similar structures, are also being developed.

(ESA), would provide the Columbus attached module, also a laboratory. Columbus is the name of Europe's space station program, which also includes free-flying platforms designed for servicing from *Freedom*. ESA is also planning its own shuttle craft to fly astronauts up to the station. Called *Hermes*, it will be launched by an Ariane 5 rocket.

Japan would provide the fourth main module, JEM (Japanese Experimental Module). This consists of a pressurized module, a robot manipulator, and an open platform for carrying equipment. Canada's contribution is a robot mobile servicing system. It will move along the beam structures and help assembly, maintenance, and servicing of the space station.

The construction of space station *Freedom* was scheduled to begin in 1995 and end in 1999. But, as problems continued to plague the space shuttle, it became unlikely that this timetable would be met. By the end of 1990, a redesign seemed necessary. The existing design appeared to be too heavy and to consume too much power. Also, too many spacewalks would be needed for servicing the station. A 1990 government advisory committee recommended simplifying the station and deemphasizing the shuttle.

Space colonies

Space stations hold the key to continued human expansion into the Solar System. They will act as bases for the construction of lunar and interplanetary craft, and as spaceports when such craft become operational. The reason is that, to reach the Moon and the planets, a spacecraft must be accelerated to at least the Earth's escape velocity, some 40,000 km/h (25,000 mph). It is much easier to do this from orbit, since the craft will already be traveling at orbital velocity, some 28,000 km/h (17,000 mph).

Astronauts will return to the Moon, probably in the early years of next century. This time the astronauts will set up a permanent base, which will eventually support a wide range of scientific and engineering activities, such as astronomy and mining. It may well be that when the Earth runs out of essential mineral ores, these may have to be imported from the Moon.

The astronauts will be ferried to the Moon in a lunar transfer vehicle, which will go into orbit. From there they will travel to and from the surface in a landing craft similar to the Apollo lunar module. To begin with, they will live in makeshift accommodations, such as spent rocket casings, partly buried by lunar soil as protection against deadly cosmic radiation. Permanent quarters will later be built using materials – metals and rock – obtained from the Moon itself. These quarters will probably be located underground for protection. Eventually, the Moon base will feature glass-domed greenhouse modules.

▼ It is early next century. A lunar ferry has just landed near the expanding Moon base. The crew will be taken there in a pressurized transporter (foreground.)

The living areas will be pressurized, using oxygen extracted from lunar rocks. Water will be precious, and will probably have to be made by combining oxygen with hydrogen imported in liquid form from the Earth. The careful recycling of raw materials will be essential.

The next goal after the Moon will be the Red Planet, Mars, the only planet in the Solar System on which human beings could survive. A trip to Mars is very much more difficult than a trip to the Moon, because it lies so far away: at least 56 million km (35 million mi.).

Even at the most favorable alignments in space of Earth and Mars, it would take a spacecraft at least 18 months for a flyby and return mission. But at other times landing missions could take two years or more. Astronauts would no doubt be able to survive physically in space for this length of time. But as yet no propulsion technology or life-support systems exist to make such a trip feasible.

▲▼ Colonizing Mars. An orbiting Mars station (below) could act as a base to support the exploration of the surface (above). These astronauts are exploring a region of Mars called Noctis Labyrinthus, the Labyrinth of the Night. It is early morning, and the canyons are coated with frost and filled with mist.

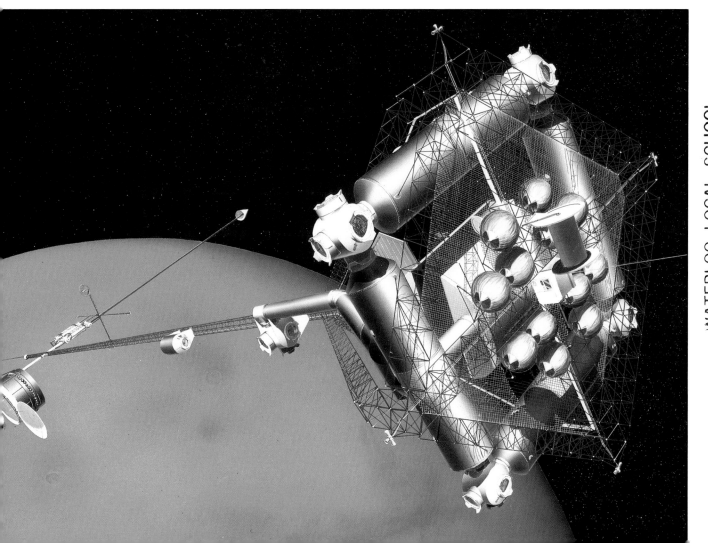

To the stars

It would not be practical to use existing chemical rockets to send astronauts to Mars. To make the journey in a reasonable time and have reserve power to cope with emergencies, a better means of propulsion is needed. One possibility is the nuclear rocket, in which the energy needed to accelerate a propellant comes from a nuclear reactor. This produces heat when uranium atoms split, or undergo fission.

Nuclear-fission energy could be applied to rocket propulsion in two ways. It could be used to accelerate a gas, such as hydrogen, to create the rocket exhaust. Or it could be used to generate an electric field, which would accelerate ions. The great advantage with the nuclear rockets is that they would develop higher thrust than chemical rockets.

Nuclear-fission engines would be suitable for speedier interplanetary journeys within our Solar System. But they would be no good for the ultimate goal of humankind, travel to the stars. The great, and at present insurmountable, problem of interstellar travel is distance. Even the nearest stars are more than 40 trillion km (25 trillion mi.) away. Existing rockets would take hundreds of thousands of years to reach them. Only if we could build rockets that could travel at speeds close to the speed of light, could we visit the stars in a reasonable time frame.

Two concepts to achieve such speeds have been put forward. Both use the technology of nuclear fusion: the conversion of hydrogen into helium, with the release of abundant energy. This is the process behind that terrible weapon, the H-bomb. One concept is the interstellar ramjet, a machine that would use hydrogen for fuel which it would scoop up from space. The other concept, the nuclear pulse rocket, would use for propulsion the gases ejected at high speed in mini H-bomb explosions.

▼ Many centuries hence, an interstellar cruise ship visits an alien planetary system to take on fuel. This "world ship" supports a vast community able to survive journeys of thousands of years.

▶ Powered by a nuclear pulse rocket, an interstellar probe called *Daedalus* passes Neptune as it accelerates out of the Solar System. This concept was put forward by the British Interplanetary Society.

Units of measurement

Units of measurement

This encyclopedia gives measurements in metric units, which are commonly used in science. Approximate equivalents in traditional American units, sometimes called U.S. customary units, are also given in the text, in parentheses.

Some common metric and U.S. units

Here are some equivalents, accurate to parts per million. For many practical purposes rougher equivalents may be adequate, especially when the quantity being converted from one system to the other is known with an accuracy of just one or two digits. Equivalents marked with an asterisk (*) are exact.

Volume
1 cubic centimeter = 0.0610237 cubic inch
1 cubic meter = 35.3147 cubic feet
1 cubic meter = 1.30795 cubic yards
1 cubic kilometer = 0.239913 cubic mile

1 cubic inch = 16.3871 cubic centimeters
1 cubic foot = 0.0283168 cubic meter
1 cubic yard = 0.764555 cubic meter

Liquid measure
1 milliliter = 0.0338140 fluidounce
1 liter = 1.05669 quarts

1 fluidounce = 29.5735 milliliters
1 quart = 0.946353 liter

Mass and weight
1 gram = 0.0352740 ounce
1 kilogram = 2.20462 pounds
1 metric ton = 1.10231 short tons

1 ounce = 28.3495 grams
1 pound = 0.453592 kilogram
1 short ton = 0.907185 metric ton

Length
1 millimeter = 0.0393701 inch
1 centimeter = 0.393701 inch
1 meter = 3.28084 feet
1 meter = 1.09361 yards
1 kilometer = 0.621371 mile

1 inch = 2.54* centimeters
1 foot = 0.3048* meter
1 yard = 0.9144* meter
1 mile = 1.60934 kilometers

Area
1 square centimeter = 0.155000 square inch
1 square meter = 10.7639 square feet
1 square meter = 1.19599 square yards
1 square kilometer = 0.386102 square mile

1 square inch = 6.4516* square centimeters
1 square foot = 0.0929030 square meter
1 square yard = 0.836127 square meter
1 square mile = 2.58999 square kilometers

1 hectare = 2.47105 acres
1 acre = 0.404686 hectare

Temperature conversions

To convert temperatures in degrees Celsius to temperatures in degrees Fahrenheit, or vice versa, use these formulas:

Celsius Temperature = (Fahrenheit Temperature − 32) × 5/9
Fahrenheit Temperature = (Celsius Temperature × 9/5) + 32

Numbers and abbreviations

Numbers

Scientific measurements sometimes involve extremely large numbers. Scientists often express large numbers in a concise "exponential" form using powers of 10. The number one billion, or 1,000,000,000, if written in this form, would be 10^9; three billion, or 3,000,000,000, would be 3×10^9. The "exponent" 9 tells you that there are nine zeros following the 3. More complicated numbers can be written in this way by using decimals; for example, 3.756×10^9 is the same as 3,756,000,000.

Very small numbers – numbers close to zero – can be written in exponential form with a minus sign on the exponent. For example, one-billionth, which is 1/1,000,000,000 or 0.000000001, would be 10^{-9}. Here, the 9 in the exponent -9 tells you that, in the decimal form of the number, the 1 is in the ninth place to the right of the decimal point. Three-billionths, or 3/1,000,000,000, would be 3×10^{-9}; accordingly, 3.756×10^{-9} would mean 0.000000003756 (or 3.756/1,000,000,000).

Here are the American names of some powers of ten, and how they are written in numerals:

1 million (10^6)	1,000,000
1 billion (10^9)	1,000,000,000
1 trillion (10^{12})	1,000,000,000,000
1 quadrillion (10^{15})	1,000,000,000,000,000
1 quintillion (10^{18})	1,000,000,000,000,000,000
1 sextillion (10^{21})	1,000,000,000,000,000,000,000
1 septillion (10^{24})	1,000,000,000,000,000,000,000,000

Principal abbreviations used in the encyclopedia

°C	degrees Celsius
cc	cubic centimeter
cm	centimeter
cu.	cubic
d	days
°F	degrees Fahrenheit
fl. oz.	fluidounce
fps	feet per second
ft.	foot
g	gram
h	hour
Hz	hertz
in.	inch
K	kelvin (degree temperature)
kg	kilogram
l	liter
lb.	pound
m	meter
mi.	mile
ml	milliliter
mm	millimeter
mph	miles per hour
mps	miles per second
mya	millions of years ago
N	north
oz.	ounce
qt.	quart
s	second
S	south
sq.	square
V	volt
y	year
yd.	yard

Glossary

aberration A defect, such as spherical aberration in lenses.

achromatic lens One made of two or more lenses of different kinds of glass, which prevent chromatic aberration, or color blurring of the image.

acid rain Rain containing acid, derived from pollutants in the atmosphere, such as sulfur dioxide.

AIDS acquired immune deficiency syndrome, a devastating disease caused by infection with human immuno deficiency virus (HIV).

alchemy An art and craft that sought to turn base metals into gold. It flourished for a thousand years in the Middle Ages, and its practitioners laid the foundations of the science of chemistry.

alternative energy Methods of producing energy other than by burning fossil fuels or by nuclear power.

alternative medicine Also called fringe medicine; treatment other than by conventional medical procedures. Examples include acupuncture (treatment with needles), and homeopathy (the use of diluted solutions of natural substances that in healthy people would produce symptoms of the disease treated).

antimatter Matter made up of antiparticles, "mirror images" of ordinary atomic particles. The positron is the antiparticle of the electron, being identical except that it has a positive rather than a negative electric charge.

antiparticle Every subatomic particle has an exact opposite, known as an antiparticle. The antiparticle of the negatively charged electron is the positron, a particle that is identical except that it has a positive electric charge.

artificial gravity A gravitational force induced, for example, by

rotating a space station.

artificial intelligence A kind of intelligence acquired by advanced computers, which allows them, for example to learn from their mistakes.

asteroids Also called minor planets; rocky bodies that circle the Sun, mostly between the orbits of Mars and Jupiter.

astronomy The scientific study of the heavens.

atom The smallest part of a chemical element that has the properties of that element.

atom smasher The popular name for a particle accelerator.

atomic clock A clock that uses the vibration of certain atoms as a regulator to measure time.

balance A sensitive weighing device. It traditionally incorporates an arm with pans hanging from each end. One is balanced against the other to measure weight.

biosphere The region of the Earth that is capable of supporting life, which includes the land (top of the lithosphere), the oceans (hydrosphere), and the lower part of the atmosphere.

biotechnology The production and use of microorganisms to make useful products, such as drugs.

black hole An awesome heavenly object is thought to result when a supermassive star dies and collapses in on itself. The star crushes itself out of existence, leaving a region of space with fantastically high gravity, which will swallow up anything nearby, including light.

bubble chamber A device used in nuclear physics for detecting subatomic particles. The particles trigger bubbles in a chamber of liquid hydrogen, maintained at a temperature near its boiling point.

burster The name given to powerful sources of gamma rays in space.

cathode-ray tube An electron tube with a fluorescent screen, on which an image is produced by the manipulation of a beam of electrons.

chip A tiny sliver of crystal, usually made of silicon, which carries thousands of miniaturized electronic circuits.

chromatography A method of separating components in a mixture. The term means "color writing." It is so called because it was originally used by the Russian botanist Mikhail Tsvet to separate color pigments in plants. In modern methods of chromatography color is not necessarily involved.

climate The average weather pattern for a region over a long period.

cloning Producing genetically identical organisms from a single ancestor, for example by means of genetic engineering.

comet A small member of the Solar System often described as a "dirty snowball" and made up of rock, ice, and dust. It releases gas and dust, and starts to shine when it approaches the Sun.

conservation Preserving something, such as resources, wildlife, habitats.

continental drift The gradual movement of the continents across the Earth's surface.

cosmic rays Penetrating radiation that reaches the Earth from space.

desalinization Removing the salt from seawater.

desertification Turning a region into desert; for example, by bad land management or overgrazing.

digital Values expressed in the form

of digits, or figures, especially the two binary digits (bits) 0 and 1.

DNA Abbreviation for "deoxyribonucleic acid," the substance making up the genes, which determine and organize the functions of the living cell.

echo sounding A detection technique using ultrasonic waves. Pulses of waves are transmitted, and their reflections, or echoes, are detected.

ecology The study of animal and plant species in relation to their environment.

electromagnetic radiation One that consists of vibrating electric and magnetic fields.

electron One of the three main stable subatomic particles, which has a mass 1/1836 that of the proton and a negative electric charge. Every atom has one or more electrons circling around a central nucleus. Electron flow constitutes an electric current.

electron microscope One that produces magnified images by the manipulation of a beam of electrons.

electronics The branch of science concerned with the manipulation and control of electrons, particularly in semiconductors and tubes, like the cathode-ray tube.

ESA The European Space Agency, the coordinating body for space activities in Europe.

extinction The elimination of a living species from the face of the Earth.

extraterrestrial Existing outside the Earth.

fission Splitting; particularly nuclear fission, the splitting of a heavy atom (usually uranium) with the release of energy.

fluorescence The property of certain materials to absorb light or other radiation of one wavelength and radiate it as light of another.

fly-by-wire A system of control in aircraft in which movements of the control stick and rudder pedals are transmitted to control surfaces not mechanically, but via electrical signals through wires, under computer guidance.

fossil fuels The "mineral" fuels: oil, natural gas, and coal, which are the remains of once-living organisms.

fusion Joining together; especially nuclear fusion, the joining together of light atoms (such as hydrogen) to make heavier ones (such as helium), with the release of energy.

galaxy A huge star system in space. The galaxy to which the Sun and all the stars in the sky belong is called the Milky Way galaxy, or simply the Galaxy.

gamma rays A form of electromagnetic radiation of very short wavelength.

Geiger counter Or Geiger-Müller counter; a device for detecting and counting charged particles and radiation.

gene The unit in living things that carries information about heredity.

genetic engineering Altering the genetic makeup of living things.

geothermal energy Energy derived from heat released in the Earth's crust; for example, from rocks in volcanic regions.

global warming Increase in the overall temperature of the Earth, due, for example, to the greenhouse effect.

green A term used to describe activities or products that are friendly to the environment.

greenhouse effect The tendency of the Earth's atmosphere to behave like a greenhouse and trap solar energy. This is being brought about by the buildup of certain gases, such as carbon dioxide and methane.

holography A kind of three-dimensional photography made possible by the use of laser light. The images are termed holograms.

information technology The principles and practice of handling and transferring information, mainly by electronic means.

infrared rays Electromagnetic radiation with a wavelength just longer than that of red light.

interplanetary Between the planets.

interstellar Between the stars.

ion An atom or group of atoms that has lost or gained one or more electrons and thus acquired a positive or negative electric charge.

isotope Most chemical elements are made up of several types of atoms that vary slightly in mass. This is because they have different numbers of neutrons in their nucleus; they all have the same number of protons. Each type is called an isotope.

laser A device that generates an intense beam of parallel light rays of nearly a single wavelength. The word is an acronym that describes how the beam is produced: light amplification by the stimulated emission of radiation.

light Electromagnetic radiation that is visible to our eyes.

liquid crystal A liquid substance that has some properties of a liquid and some of a solid. The liquid crystal in, say, a calculator display twists the plane of polarization of light when electrically stimulated.

LSI Abbreviation for "large scale integration," the process of cramming more and more electronic components on a chip.

maglev Short for "magnetic levitation," an electromagnetic means of raising trains a few centimeters above the track so that friction with the track is eliminated.

meteoroid A piece of rock that hurtles through space. Small meteoroids bombard the Earth all the time, becoming visible as meteors when they burn up in the night sky. Large ones may survive and fall to the ground as meteorites.

MHD Abbreviation for "magnetohydrodynamics," a method of generating electricity using the flow of hot ionized gases.

microcircuits Miniaturized electronic circuits, formed usually in silicon chips.

microcomputer A computer based on silicon chips carrying microscopic electronic components.

microelectronics The production and application of miniaturized electronic circuits.

microorganisms Organisms of microscopic size, such as bacteria and viruses.

microwaves Electromagnetic radiation intermediate in wavelength between infrared rays and radio waves.

moving-coil instrument One that has a coil located in a magnetic field. When current passes through the coil, the magnetism set up interacts with the existing field, causing the coil to move. Most loudspeakers as well as ammeters are moving-coil devices.

MRI Abbreviation for "magnetic resonance imaging," a method of producing images that exploits the spinning of atoms and their response to radiation of certain frequencies when in a strong magnetic field.

NASA The National Aeronautics and Space Administration, the body that coordinates space activities in the United States.

neutron One of the three main subatomic particles, present in every atomic nucleus except that of the ordinary hydrogen atom. It has a similar mass to the other particle in the nucleus, the proton, but no electric charge.

neutron star A very dense body that results when a star several times heavier than the Sun dies. It is made of neutrons, may be only a few tens of kilometers across, and usually rotates rapidly.

nuclear energy Energy derived from the nuclei of atoms. It can be released by the fission or fusion of the atoms.

nucleus The central part of an atom, which contains the bulk of the atom's mass. It contains neutrons and protons (in ordinary hydrogen, just a proton) and has a positive electric charge.

orbit The path through space of one body around another, such as a satellite circling around the Earth.

organic farming A method of farming without the use of pesticide sprays or man-made fertilizers.

oscilloscope A cathode-ray tube instrument used to display varying electrical quantities or phenomena that can be expressed through them.

OTEC Abbreviation for "ocean thermal energy conversion," a futuristic method of extracting heat from the oceans.

particle accelerator Or atom smasher; a machine for accelerating charged particles to high speed in order to bombard atoms or other particles.

pesticide A preparation that kills pests, including insecticides to kill insects, fungicides to kill fungus diseases, and herbicides to kill weeds.

plate theory Or plate tectonics; the theory that the Earth's crust and upper mantle is made up of many plates, or segments, which slowly move because of convection currents in the fluid rocks underneath.

polarized light Light that vibrates in only one plane. Ordinary light vibrates in many planes.

pollution The poisoning of the environment: land, sea, and air.

probe A spacecraft that escapes from the Earth's gravity and travels to the Moon, the planets, or other heavenly bodies.

propfan An advanced aircraft engine that has a specially shaped, fanlike propeller.

proton One of the three main subatomic particles. Protons are found in the nuclei of all atoms, and have a positive electric charge.

pulsar A heavenly body that emits pulses of radiation, such as X-rays, radio waves, and light. Pulsars are thought to be rapidly rotating neutron stars.

qualitative analysis A form of chemical analysis that tries to identify the substances present in a sample, classically by step-by-step treatment with a variety of chemical reagents.

quantitative analysis A form of chemical analysis concerned with finding the quantities of substances present in a sample. Titration against standard solutions is a classic quantitative method.

quasars Quasi-stellar objects; starlike heavenly bodies that lie far away in space. They appear to be very much smaller than galaxies, but very much brighter.

radar A method of locating objects, such as aircraft, by bouncing pulses of radio waves off them. The word stands for "radio detection and ranging."

radiation A stream of energetic particles or electromagnetic radiation, such as alpha particles or gamma rays.

radio telescope A device designed to pick up radio waves coming from the heavens. Most radio telescopes gather the waves in huge dishes, which reflect them onto a receiving antenna.

radio waves A form of electromagnetic radiation with long wavelengths.

radiography Producing images using radiation, such as X-rays.

radioisotope A radioactive isotope; an isotope whose atoms are unstable and give off radiation.

range finder A device that measures the range, or distance, to an object. Some recent ones use laser beams.

recycling Processing and using again materials already used once.

red shift The shift of dark lines in the spectrum of stars and galaxies toward the red end of the spectrum. It is interpreted as a Doppler effect, the lengthening of wavelengths of light from a source moving away. Astronomers can use the red shift to calculate the speed of recession of the star or galaxy. For galaxies, which travel faster the farther they are away, this also enables their distance to be measured.

reflector An astronomical telescope that gathers and focuses light by means of mirrors.

refractor An astronomical telescope that gathers and focuses light by means of lenses.

regulator The device in a timepiece that undergoes a regular cycle; used as a yardstick to measure the passage of time.

relativity A theory propounded by the scientist Albert Einstein that seeks to explain the nature of time, space, matter, and energy, and the relationships between them.

resolution Or resolving power; the extent to which a microscope or telescope can separate objects close together.

robot A machine or device that can be programmed to imitate human actions and replace humans in some situations.

satellite A small body that orbits around another in space; artificial satellites have been launched around the Earth.

semiconductor A material that is neither a true conductor of electricity nor an insulator. Electricity can be made to flow through it under certain conditions.

SETI Abbreviation for "search for extraterrestrial intelligence," the name given to projects that are on the lookout for radio signals from the heavens that could indicate the presence of intelligent beings.

solar energy Energy derived from the Sun.

sonar A means of underwater detection and communication using sound waves; a kind of sound radar.

space station A large, permanently occupied spacecraft in orbit around the Earth.

spectroscope An instrument that splits up light or other radiation into a spectrum and allows study of this spectrum. A spectrograph is similar but records the spectrum.

spectrum The spread of colors, or wavelengths, obtained when white light is split by passage through a prism or diffraction grating. Other forms of radiation may also reveal a spectrum when suitably split.

subatomic particles Particles

smaller than the atom. There are three main stable subatomic particles: electrons, protons, and neutrons. Other subatomic particles can be produced in atom smashers. They are mostly very short-lived.

superconductor A material that has no resistance to electricity. Several materials lose their resistance when they are cooled to very low temperatures.

synchrotron A kind of circular atom smasher in which particles are accelerated by the rhythmic, or synchronized, application of an electric field.

time lag The time it takes radio signals to travel between Earth and a distant space probe, which can be a matter of hours.

tomography An X-ray imaging technique that shows details of the tissues and organs in a "slice" of the body.

transducer A device that converts one form of energy into another. Many sensing and measuring devices are transducers. For example, measurement of a physical property of a material might be translated into electrical signals.

UFO Abbreviation for "unidentified flying object," an object traveling through the sky, whose existence cannot at first readily be explained. Some people believe UFOs come from another world in space.

ultrasound Sound waves with a frequency, or pitch, too high for the ear to detect.

ultraviolet rays Electromagnetic waves with wavelengths just shorter than light rays: beyond the violet end of the spectrum.

Universe All that exists; space and all it contains.

X-rays Electromagnetic waves with wavelengths shorter than ultraviolet rays but longer than gamma rays.

Biographies

Listed here are some of the most important scientists and inventors in history.

Ampère, André Marie (1775–1836), French physicist and mathematician. Made important discoveries in electricity and magnetism. The common unit of electric current is named after him.

Aristotle (384–322 BC), ancient Greek philosopher. Wide-ranging thinker who made contributions to astronomy, meteorology, physics, and psychology, but was particularly notable for his observations and theories in biology.

Babbage, Charles (1792–1871), English mathematician. Forerunner of modern computer science. He designed what would have been, if completed, the first automatic digital computer.

Baekeland, Leo Hendrik (1863–1944), Belgian-born American chemist. Invented Velox photographic paper and Bakelite—the first completely synthetic plastic.

Bardeen, John (1908–1991), American physicist. Shared Nobel Prizes in physics for the invention of the transistor (with William Shockley and Walter Brattain) and for the development of a theory explaining superconductivity (with Leon Cooper and John Schrieffer).

Becquerel, Antoine (1852–1908), French physicist. Sometimes called the father of atomic physics for his discovery of radioactivity, in uranium.

Bohr, Niels (1885–1962), Danish physicist. Enormously influential in the development of quantum physics, the basic modern theory of small-scale physical phenomena. He developed an important model for the structure of the atom.

Brahe, Tycho (1546–1601), Danish astronomer. Performed the most accurate astronomical observations of the era before the telescope. His discovery of a supernova undermined the widespread belief that the stars are perfect and unchanging.

Brown, Robert (1773–1858), Scottish botanist. Discovered the nucleus in living cells, as well as the random movements of microscopic particles suspended in a liquid or gas—now called Brownian motion.

Cavendish, Henry (1731–1810), English physicist and chemist. Did important work on gases and electricity, and made an accurate determination of the density of the Earth. The famous Cavendish Laboratory at Cambridge University in England is named for him.

Copernicus, Nicolaus (1473–1543), Polish astronomer. Put forth the revolutionary theory that the Earth is not the center of the universe but revolves, with the other planets, around the Sun.

Curie, Marie [born Maria Skłodowska] (1867–1934), Polish-born French physicist. Performed significant early research on radioactivity, discovering, with her husband, Pierre Curie (1859–1906), the elements polonium and radium. She won two Nobel Prizes—one jointly with her husband and Becquerel.

Cuvier, Georges, Baron (1769–1832), French naturalist. Carried out pioneering work in comparative anatomy and in paleontology, and proposed a detailed classification of the animal kingdom.

Dalton, John (1766–1844), English chemist. Formulated an atomic theory of matter, made major discoveries concerning the properties of gases, did extensive work in meteorology, and produced the first detailed study of color blindness, now sometimes called daltonism.

Darwin, Charles (1809–1882), English naturalist. Originated the theory of evolution of living things, including humans, by natural selection. He also made contributions to geology, developing a theory of coral reefs, and to botany, and did pioneering work on animal behavior and ecology.

Davy, Humphrey (1778–1829), English chemist. Discovered several chemical elements and compounds, and made significant findings in electrochemistry. He discovered the anesthetic effects of laughing gas, devised the first arc lamp, and invented the miner's safety lamp.

De Forest, Lee (1873–1961), American inventor. Opened the way for the flowering of electronics with his invention of the "audion" vacuum tube, featuring a "grid" permitting control of the current.

Edison, Thomas Alva (1847–1931), American inventor. Patented over 1,000 inventions, including the incandescent electric lamp and the phonograph.

His discovery of the Edison effect—the "thermionic" emission of electrons from heated materials—later provided the basis for the electron tube.

Ehrlich, Paul (1854–1915), German medical scientist. Trailblazer in the study of the blood and of immunity to disease, as well as in the development of so-called chemotherapy—the use of chemical substances to fight disease. He discovered the first effective drug treatment for syphilis.

Einstein, Albert (1879–1955), German-American physicist. Introduced the revolutionary theory of relativity, along with the idea of the equivalence of mass and energy, played a key role in the development of quantum theory, and put forth a theory of Brownian motion. He received a Nobel Prize for his work on the photoelectric effect.

Faraday, Michael (1791–1867), English physicist and chemist. Made crucial discoveries in electricity and magnetism, and developed basic laws of electrolysis. His name is remembered in the farad, a unit of electrical capacitance.

Fermi, Enrico (1901–1954), Italian-born

American physicist. Produced radioactive substances by bombarding elements with neutrons, and directed the construction of the first nuclear reactor and the achievement of the first controlled chain reaction. Element number 100, fermium, was named in his honor.

Fleming, Alexander (1881–1955), Scottish bacteriologist. Discovered penicillin, thus opening the era of antibiotics in medicine.

Franklin, Benjamin (1706–1790), American statesman, scientist, and inventor. Made notable contributions to such fields as oceanography and meteorology, as well as the study of electricity—where he introduced the principle of conservation of charge, showed that lightning is electrical in nature, and invented the lightning rod. He also was responsible for the rocking chair, bifocal glasses, the Franklin stove, and the idea of daylight saving time.

Freud, Sigmund (1856–1939), Austrian physician and neurologist. Founder of the psychoanalytic school of psychiatry.

Gabor, Dennis (1900–1979), Hungarian-born British physicist and engineer. Invented holography.

Galen (129–200), ancient Greek physician. Father of experimental physiology. He did extensive research in anatomy, and his works were standard texts for centuries.

Galilei, Galileo (1564–1642), Italian astronomer and physicist. Founder of modern mechanics (the physics of motion) and of experimental physics. He was the first to use the telescope to study the sky, and was punished by the Inquisition of the Roman Catholic Church for his support of the Copernican theory of the Solar System.

Gibbs, Josiah (1839–1903), American mathematical physicist. Foremost U.S. scientist before the 20th century. He applied thermodynamics to chemistry, created vector analysis, and did research in statistical mechanics and optics.

Goddard, Robert (1882–1945), American rocketry pioneer. Launched the first liquid-fueled rocket, and obtained 200 rocketry patents.

Halley, Edmond (1656–1742), English astronomer. Compiled a catalog of the stars of the Southern Hemisphere, calculated the orbits of numerous comets, and showed that stars are not fixed but in motion. Halley's comet is named for him.

Harvey, William (1578–1657), English physician. Discovered how the blood circulates, and the function of the heart as a pump.

Heisenberg, Werner (1901–1976), German physicist. Quantum mechanics pioneer whose famous uncertainty principle held that the position and momentum of a particle cannot both be determined at the same time with any certainty.

Helmholtz, Hermann von (1821–1894), German physicist and physiologist. Did important research in electrodynamics, and formulated the principle of conservation of energy. He studied the nervous system, hearing, and vision, and invented the ophthalmoscope.

Herschel, William (1738–1822), German-born English astronomer. Discovered the planet Uranus, cataloged 2,500 nebulae and star clusters, and showed that the Solar System moves through space and that binary stars revolve around each other. He constructed several large telescopes.

Hertz, Heinrich (1857–1894), German physicist. Was the first to transmit and receive radio waves, and showed that light consists of electromagnetic waves. The basic unit of wave frequency is now called the hertz.

Hubble, Edwin (1889–1953), American astronomer. Established that some nebulae are galaxies outside our own Galaxy, and that they are receding from us—that is, the universe is expanding.

Humboldt, Alexander, Baron von (1769–1859), German naturalist. Made fundamental contributions to physical geography, biogeography, botany, climatology, and geophysics. He conducted major expeditions in the Americas and Central Asia.

Hutton, James (1726–1797), Scottish geologist. Founder of modern geology. He originated the theory that the features of the Earth's crust are due to natural processes that are still occurring.

Huygens, Christiaan (1629–1695), Dutch

mathematician, astronomer, and physicist. Founded the wave theory of light, showed that Saturn is surrounded by rings, and invented the pendulum clock.

Jenner, Edward (1749–1823), English physician. Established vaccination on a scientific basis with his work on smallpox.

Joule, Robert Prescott (1818–1889), British physicist. Determined the amount of mechanical energy producing a unit of heat, and showed how the heat generated by an electric current in a wire depends on the wire's resistance and the current. The joule, a standard unit of work and energy, is named after him.

Kamerlingh Onnes, Heike (1853–1926), Dutch physicist. Liquefied helium, and discovered superconductivity.

Kekulé von Stradonitz, Friedrich (1829–1896), German chemist. Laid the foundations for the structural theory of organic chemistry—the chemistry of most compounds containing carbon. He established the ring structure of benzene.

Kelvin, Lord [William Thomson] (1824–1907), Scottish physicist and

inventor. Made important contributions to the study of thermodynamics and electricity and to the development of telegraphy. He proposed the absolute temperature scale, whose basic unit, the kelvin, is named after him.

Kepler, Johannes (1571–1630), German astronomer. Established that the planets move in elliptical orbits, and founded the modern science of optics.

Koch, Robert (1843–1910), German physician. Discovered the bacteria that cause anthrax, tuberculosis, and cholera, and helped create the science of bacteriology.

Lamarck, Jean-Baptiste de Monet, chevalier de (1744–1829), French biologist. Evolutionist who held that plants and animals acquire characteristics required by their environment and that these characteristics can be inherited. He founded modern invertebrate zoology, and introduced the word "biology."

Lavoisier, Antoine (1743–1794), French chemist. Father of modern chemistry. He applied quantitative methods to chemistry, distinguished between elements and compounds, provided a

chemical explanation of combustion in place of the old phlogiston theory, and studied respiration.

Lawrence, Ernest Orlando (1901–1958), American physicist. Invented the cyclotron, the first high-energy particle accelerator. Element 103, lawrencium, was named in his honor.

Leonardo da Vinci (1452–1519), Italian artist, scientist, and inventor. Contributed to an amazing range of fields, including anatomy, architecture, military engineering, and geology. He designed machine tools, irrigation systems, a paddle-wheel boat, a horseless carriage, and a flying machine, and invented the parachute.

Linnaeus, Carolus (1707–1778), Swedish naturalist. Established the modern "binomial" (using genus and species) system for naming living organisms.

Lorenz, Edward (1917–   ), American meteorologist. Played a key role in the development of chaos theory, which finds orderly patterns in many seemingly irregular phenomena.

Lorenz, Konrad (1903–1989), Austrian

zoologist. Trailblazing researcher of animal behavior and communication.

Marconi, Guglielmo (1874–1937), Italian electrical engineer. Pioneered in the development of radio communication. His transmission of a radio signal across the Atlantic produced a worldwide sensation.

Maxwell, James Clerk (1831–1879), Scottish physicist. Greatest theoretical physicist of the 19th century. He performed important research on electricity and magnetism, formulated the basic electromagnetic theory of light, analyzed the behavior of gas molecules, and did fundamental work on the perception and composition of colors.

McClintock, Barbara (1902–   ), American geneticist. Discovered that certain genetic elements— "jumping genes"—could change positions on a chromosome, triggering changes in the activity of other genes.

Mendel, Gregor (1822–1884), Austrian botanist and monk. Discovered the basic laws of heredity through research on pea plants.

Mendeleev, Dmitri Ivanovich (1834–1907), Russian chemist. Formulated a classification of the chemical elements— the Periodic Table— reflecting similarities in their properties. Element number 101, mendelevium, was named in his honor.

Morgan, Thomas Hunt (1866–1945), American zoologist and geneticist. Working with fruit flies, established the chromosome theory of heredity, with genes arranged in a row on chromosomes.

Newton, Isaac (1642–1727), English physicist, astronomer, and mathematician. Formulated the three basic laws of motion, put forth a theory of universal gravitation, and discovered calculus. He showed that white light is composed of a mixture of colors, and invented the reflecting telescope.

Pasteur, Louis (1822–1895), French chemist and microbiologist. Proved that microorganisms cause fermentation and disease, showed that microorganisms do not arise by "spontaneous generation," introduced pasteurization, and developed a rabies vaccine.

Pauling, Linus (1901–   ), American chemist. Applied quantum mechanics to chemistry, and made important discoveries about molecular structure and chemical bonds.

Pavlov, Ivan Petrovich (1849–1936), Russian physiologist. Studied the nervous system's control of the heart and the pancreas, investigated secretions of digestive glands, and developed the concept of the conditioned reflex.

Planck, Max (1858–1947), German physicist. Father of quantum theory.

Priestley, Joseph (1733–1804), English chemist. Discovered oxygen and several other gases, and performed experiments in electricity.

Roentgen, Wilhelm (1845–1923), German physicist. Discovered X-rays, for which he received the first Nobel Prize in physics.

Russell, Henry Norris (1877–1957), American astronomer. Did work on binary stars and stellar evolution. Along with the Dane Ejnar Hertzsprung, he found a relation between the spectral types and luminosity of stars.

Rutherford, Ernest (1871–1937), New Zealand-born British physicist. Studied radioactivity, discovered alpha and beta rays, showed that an atom has a nucleus with positive charge and most of the atom's mass, and achieved the first artificial transmutation of an element.

Seaborg, Glenn (1912–   ), American chemist. Synthesized and identified several elements beyond uranium in the Periodic Table.

Skinner, B. F. (1904–1990), American behavioral psychologist. Experimented in "operant conditioning" of animals to show that behavior is largely determined by positive and negative reinforcements in the environment. He developed teaching machines applying his ideas of programmed learning.

Stanley, Wendell (1904–1971), American biochemist. Discovered that viruses can be crystallized, thus making it possible to determine their structure.

Staudinger, Hermann (1881–1965), German chemist. Pioneered in the study of polymerization.

Tesla, Nikola (1856–1943), Serbian-American inventor. Discovered the rotating magnetic field, basic to alternating-current machines, and pioneered in electric power transmission and radio. The tesla, a unit of magnetic flux density, is named for him.

Thomson, Joseph John (1856–1940), British physicist. Discovered the electron.

Townes, Charles (1915–   ), American physicist. Invented the maser, a device that emits microwaves just as the laser, which came later, emits light.

Tsiolkovski, Konstantin Eduardovich (1857–1935), Russian aeronautic and astronautic scientist. Did extensive theoretical work in rocket engineering and space flight.

Vesalius, Andreas (1514–1564), Belgian physician. Known as the father of modern anatomy for his accurate anatomy work based on dissection of human cadavers, rather than animals.

Volta, Alessandro (1745–1827), Italian physicist. Invented the voltaic pile (the first electric battery), and discovered methane. The unit of potential difference called the volt is named for him.

Watson, James (1928–   ), American molecular biologist. With the British biophysicist Francis Crick, discovered the molecular structure of DNA.

Watt, James (1736–1819), Scottish engineer. Helped power the Industrial Revolution with his improvements in the steam engine. A standard unit of power, the watt, is named after him.

Wegener, Alfred (1880–1930), German geophysicist and meteorologist. Originated the idea of continental drift.

Whitney, Eli (1765–1825), American inventor and manufacturer. Invented the cotton gin, and helped develop mass production by using standardized tools and interchangeable parts.

Wright, Orville (1871–1948) and **Wilbur** (1867–1912). American aviation pioneers. Brothers who designed and built the first passenger-carrying heavier-than-air aircraft to achieve powered flight.

Young, Thomas (1773–1829), English physician and physicist. Demonstrated interference of light, thereby establishing that light consists of waves. He contributed to the study of elasticity, color perception, and the eyes.

Index

This Index covers all 12 volumes of the encyclopedia. In the entries, a dark, or "boldfaced," number followed by a colon is a volume number; the lighter number or numbers after the colon are page numbers. For example, **2**:16; **5**:28, 79 means page 16 of Volume 2 and pages 28 and 79 of Volume 5. Page numbers in *italics* refer to pictures. Users of this Index should note that information about many scientists is in the Biographies section preceding the Index. Also, in each volume explanations of many scientific terms can be found in the volume's Glossary.

A

anglerfish **7**:16, *16*
Anglo-Nubian goat **7**:74, *75*
Angora goat **7**:74
annealing **8**:56
Annelida **5**:21
annulus **2**:50
anode **1**:52, 53, *55*
Antarctic Ocean **3**:50, *50*
Antarctica **3**:76, 85; **12**:51
antelope **3**:79; **4**:*65*; **5**:56, 67, 72, 72, 83
antenna **11**:32, 34, 35
anthracite **9**:10, 12, 13
antibiotics **6**:47, 72, 74; **12**:58, 59
antibodies **6**:64, 68, 69, 76
anticline **9**:18, *19*
antigens **6**:69
antipyrine **6**:75
antlers **5**:72
Antlia **2**:*30*
ants **4**:62; **5**:24, *67*, 81; **11**:*53*
anus **6**:24, *24*
aperture synthesis **12**:31
aphelion **3**:14
aphids **5**:81
Aphrodite Terra **2**:57
Apollo 8 **2**:47
Apollo 11 **2**:78, 80
Apollo 14 **9**:81
Apollo 17 **2**:81
Apollo EVA suit **10**:75, *75*
Apollo Moon-landing project **2**:78, 81; **10**:58, 60-61, *61*, *62*, 74, 78; **12**:49
Apollo-Soyuz Test Project (ASTP) **10**:63
apparent magnitude **2**:16
Aquarius **2**:11, *24*
aquifer **3**:*59*
Aquila **2**:13
Arabian Desert **3**:84
Arabian oryx **7**:*34*
arachnids **5**:26
Aral Sea **7**:25
arc welding **8**:9
arctic fox **5**:41
Arctic Circle **9**:23
Arctic Ocean **3**:50, *50*
arctic tern **5**:74, 76
Arecibo radio telescope **12**:31, 78
arête **3**:*42*
Argentina **7**:72; **9**:52

Argiope bruennichi **5**:27
argon **3**:63, 66; **8**:17; **8**:62
Argyre Basin **2**:58, 60, *60*
Ariane 3 **9**:84, *84*
Ariane 5 **12**:81
Aries **2**:13
Arkwright, Richard **8**:49, 50
Arles Merino sheep **7**:*72*
armadillos **5**:52
armalcolite **2**:78
Armstrong, Neil **10**:58, 60
aromatics **8**:42
arteries **6**:15, *15*, 16, 52; **12**:63
artesian **3**:*59*
arthritis **6**:73, 81
arthropod **4**:15, 19, 39; **5**:26, 27
articulated vehicles **10**:19
artificial insemination **7**:52
asbestos **8**:13, 22
Ascraeus Mons **2**:58
asexual reproduction **4**:54, 55, *55*
ash (tree) **3**:80
Asia **3**:80; **7**:56
asphalt **9**:18, 24
aspirin **1**:18; **6**:72; **7**:70, 77
assembly line **8**:51
astatine **1**:28
asteroids **2**:58, 72, 73
    belt of **2**:63
    orbits of **2**:74, 75
    size of **2**:74, 75
asthenosphere **3**:12, 16, *17*
asthma **6**:66, 68
astrology **2**:12, 13
astronauts **2**:79
astronomy **2**:8, 9; **11**:74; **12**:13, 25
astrophotography **11**:14
Atari **11**:70
Atlantic Ocean **3**:50; **11**:27, 31
Atlantis **10**:66
Atlas-Centaur rocket **10**:48
atmosphere, Earth's **3**:60, 62-67; **7**:23, 40; **10**:49, *49*
    composition of **3**:*64*, *65*, *67*
    saturated **3**:60
    structure of **3**:64
atmospheric pressure **3**:64, 69, 70
atoll **3**:52
atom smasher *see particle accelerator*
atomic bomb **1**:*27*; **9**:28
atomic number **1**:30

atomic structure **1**:19, 20
atomic theories **1**:19
atoms **1**:18, 26, 49; **11**:77
    charged **1**:*33*
    particles in **1**:*21*, 24, *24*
    structure of **9**:*28*
atria **6**:16, *16*, *58*
Auriger **2**:13
aurochs **7**:65, *67*
aurora **3**:*65*
Aurora Borealis **2**:50
Australia **1**:82; **2**:34, 57, 76, 77; **4**:32, *44*, *45*; **5**:20, 26, 28, 36, 37, 40, 41, 55, 77; **7**:*23*, 64, 65, 70, 72; **8**:8, 11, 21; **9**:8, 9, 13, 32, 36, 40, 47, 74; **10**:55, *61*, *62*; **12**:29
Australian Current **3**:50
Australian mountain ash **4**:62
Australian shield bug **4**:*57*
australoid race **4**:32, *32*
Australopithecus afarensis **4**:27, 28, *28*
automata **11**:81
automatic pilot **11**:80
automation **11**:81
automobile **8**:47, 82, 83; **10**: 7, 14, 16-17
    see also car assembly, car design, electric cars
auxins **4**:79
avalanche **3**:*42*
aviation fuel **9**:16
avocet **7**:*11*
axon **4**:52, 53; **6**:29, *29*
azurite **8**:11

B

Babbage, Charles **11**:52
baboon **5**:62, *62*, 72, 82, 83
Babylon **2**:12
Babylonian astronomy **12**:14
bacon-type hogs **7**:71
bacteria **3**:*66*; **4**:65; **5**:8, 9, *9*; **6**:16, 23, 35, 62, 64, 75; **7**:12
Baekeland, Leo **8**:39, *39*
Baikonur Cosmodrome **9**:85; **10**:63, *63*, 65
Bailly **2**:78
Baird, John Logie **11**:34
Bakelite **8**:39, *39*, 66, 68

M

Maiman, Theodore H. 1:74; **12**:42

mainframe computers **11**:54, *54*, 60, *60*

maize **7**:49, *53*, 54, 55, 56, *56*

makeup **11**:72

malachite **8**:11

malaria **6**:73; **12**:59

Malaysia **7**:60, 80; **8**:20

Mallard **10**:21

mallards **5**:60, *60*

malnutrition **6**:53; **12**:59

Mamber goat **7**:*75*

mammals **4**:14, 20, 22, 24, 60-61, 74, 75; **5**:40-45
    classification of **5**:*40*
    courtship in **5**:59
    defense in **5**:54
    gestures in **5**:70
    hibernation in **5**:75
    migration in **5**:78
    parenthood in **5**:64
    scent in **5**:67

Manarov, Musa **10**:70

mandrill **5**:*59*

manganese **8**:30

manganese dioxide **1**:53

manganese nodules **8**:16, 27

mango **7**:*58*

mangosteen **7**:*58*

mankind *see humankind*

manned maneuvering unit (MMU) **10**:76, 77

mantis **4**:39, *39*

mantle, Earth's **3**:8, 16, 17, 22, *22*, 24

manufacturing **8**:47; **12**:8, 56

maple **3**:80

mapping, of genes **12**:*64*

marble **8**:22

Marconi, Guglielmo **11**:31, *31*, 32

margarine **7**:60; **8**:62, 74, 75

marginal crevasse **3**:*42*

maria **2**:55

Marianas Trench **3**:77

Mariner 2 **10**:54

Mariner 10 **2**:55, 56, 60

Mariner Valley **2**:58, 60

marmots **5**:68, 75

Mars **2**:52, *54*, 58, 59, *59*; **10**:54, *54*; **12**:83
    atmosphere of **2**:*59*
    ice on **2**:*61*

moons of **2**:82
    orbit of **2**:*53*
    seasons on **2**:58
    structure of **2**:*58*
    surface of **2**:*54*, 60, *61*
    weather on **2**:*60*

marsupials **4**:*42*; **5**:40, 41

martens **5**:51

mass production **8**:48, 51; **12**:13

mass spectroscopy **12**:34, 37

mathematics **11**:49, 50, 60

mating **5**:59, 61

matte **8**:32

matter **1**:8; **2**:42

Mauna Kea Observatory **12**:28

Mauritius **7**:31

Maxwell, James Clerk **1**:76, 77

Mayall reflector **12**:24

mayfly **7**:*13*

McCandless, Bruce **10**:70, *76*

McMath telescope **12**:*28*

measles **6**:76; **12**:59

measurement **12**:8
    of distance **12**:12
    of length **12**:12
    of temperature **12**:17
    of time **12**:8, 14, 15
    of weight **12**:8, 10, 11

meat-eating plants **5**:19, *19*

mechanical excavator **9**:12, *13*

medicine **6**:72-85; **11**:62, 76; **12**:58, 59
    preventative **12**:59

Mediterranean Sea **7**:32, 45; **9**:23, 34

medulla, of brain **6**:*32*

medulla, of kidney **6**:27

meerkat **5**:*80*

megabit **11**:54

megaflop **11**:48

Megalosaurus **4**:*22*

Mège Mouriès, Hipployte **8**:74

melanin **6**:9

melting **1**:11, 16

meltwater **3**:*42*

memory **6**:35, 38, 39
    computer **11**:49, 50, 52, 55, 63, 68

meninges **6**:35, *35*

meningitis **6**:35

mental illness **6**:61

menthol crystals **1**:7

Merbold, Ulf **10**:78, 83, *83*

Mercury **2**:24, 52, 54, 55, *55*; **3**:9
    orbit of **2**:*53*
    structure of **2**:*55*
    surface of **2**:*55*

mercury **1**:12, 28, *55*; **8**:34; **9**:62; **11**:15

Mercury spacecraft **10**:58, 59, *71*

Merino sheep **7**:72, *72*

mesopause **3**:64

Mesozoic **4**:22

Messier, Charles **2**:33

metallic bond **1**:*35*

metals **1**:32; **8**:9, 34, 35, 54-61
    joining of **8**:58-59
    native **8**:10, *10*

metamorphic rock
    regional **3**:36
    thermal **3**:36
    see also rock

metamorphosis **4**:47

meteor **2**:72, 76

Meteor Crater **2**:72, 76

meteorite **2**:52, 72, *72*, 76, 83; **4**:8
    composition of **2**:77
    Martian **2**:60

meteoroid **2**:52, 76

meteorology **3**:68, 72; **10**:48

Meteosat **10**:51

meter **12**:8, 9

methane **1**:36; **2**:70, 71; **8**:25; **9**:18, 19, 24; **12**:48, 51, 56

Mexico **7**:41, 49, 62; **8**:13

Mexico, Gulf of **5**:74

mica **3**:32, 41

Michaux, Ernest and Pierre **10**:12

microbalance **12**:11

microbiology **12**:58
    see also biotechnology

microchip **8**:*84*; **11**:52, 53, 54

microcircuits **11**:52

microcomputers **11**:54, 56-57, 65, 66, 68

microfiche **11**:14

Micrographia **12**:19

micrometeoroids **10**:74

micrometeorology **3**:72

micrometer caliper **12**:9, 12

microphone **11**:24, *25*, 39, 65
    condenser **11**:39
    dynamic **11**:39

microprocessors **11**:54, 68; **12**:*66*

116

power shovels **9**:12
power train **10**:14, *14-15*
powerboat **10**:32
prairie **3**:79; **7**:20, 29
praying mantis **5**:51
predators **5**:49, 50; **7**:12, 17
preening **5**:61
pregnancy **4**:60; **6**:44-45
prehistoric animals **4**:8, 9
prehistoric art **4**:*31*
prehistoric people **4**:30
premature babies **6**:78
premolars **6**:*23*
pressure ridge **3**:*42*
pressurized-water nuclear reactor
    9:30, *30*, 31; **10**:34
prey **5**:48, 49, 50
primates **4**:24; **5**:45; **7**:32
printing **11**:7, 8-13
    colors in **11**:10
    from computers **11**:57, *57*, 68
    methods of **11**:12
    of pictures **11**:12
    of text **11**:9
prism **1**:40, *66*
Procamelus **4**:24
programs **11**:51, 57, 64, 65, 71
    RAM **11**:51
    ROM **11**:51
Progress **10**:79
prokaryotes **4**:10
prominences **2**:*51*
pronghorn antelopes **3**:*78*
propane **9**:19, 22
propellants **8**:17; **10**:67
proper motion **2**:17
propfan engine **12**:*77*
    see also jet engine
prospecting **8**:14-15
prostate gland **6**:*41*
protein **4**:*49*, 51, 67; **6**:22, 50
Proton rocket **9**:84
protons **1**:18, 20, 49; **2**:50; **9**:28
proto-planet theory **3**:*10*
protozoa **4**:10, 50; **5**:8, 9, 21
Proxima Centauri **2**:8
Przewalski's horse **7**:*34*
puffball **5**:54
puffer **5**:54
pulmonary artery **6**:*15*, *16*
pulmonary vein **6**:*16*
pulp, of tooth **6**:*23*

pulsar **2**:24, 28
pulse code modulation (PCM) **11**:26
pumice **1**:8
pumped-storage hydro plant **9**:40
punched cards **11**:81
Pup **2**:24
pupa, in insects **5**:24
pupil, of eye **6**:30, *30*, *56*
purchasing **11**:68
pyramidal peak **3**:*42*
pyrites **3**:*37*; **8**:12
pyroxine **3**:32
python **5**:28

Q

quarks **1**:20, 22; **12**:45
quarrying **8**:22
quartz **1**:10; **3**:33, *37*, 41; **8**:12;
    11:27; **12**:14
quasar **1**:*84*; **2**:9, 36-37, 40, 41, 43;
    12:25
Quaternary **4**:24
Queen Mary **8**:54, *59*
queleas **5**:80
quills **5**:52
quinine **8**:77

R

rabbit **4**:*60*; **5**:52, 68; **7**:64
raccoon **5**:42; **7**:36
races of humans **4**:32-33
racing bicycle **10**:11, *11*
racing cars **10**:8
rack-and-pinion **10**:26; **12**:11
radar **2**:56, 60; **9**:63; **10**:52; **11**:74;
    12:40
radial motion **2**:17
radiation **1**:24, 40; **2**:43, 50; **6**:71;
    9:27; **12**:38
    fireball **2**:43
radiative zone **2**:*51*
radio **11**:7, 32-34
radio astronomy **12**:30
radio beams **2**:56
radio, CB **1**:*77*
radio galaxies **2**:34
radio receiver **11**:25, 26
radio, shortwave **1**:*77*

radio signals **1**:62
radio telescope **12**:25, 30, 31
radio waves **1**:76; **10**:50; **11**:31, 74,
    75; **12**:25, 30, 37, 60
    interstellar **2**:22
    Jupiter's **2**:63
    pulsar **2**:28
    quasi-stellar **2**:36
    stellar **2**:30, 31
    Sun's **2**:49
radio window **12**:31
radioactive waste **9**:29
radioactivity **1**:24-25; **9**:26, 27, 29,
    30, 52
radiocarbon dating **1**:24, *25*
radioisotope **12**:38
radiomicrophone **11**:30
radiotherapy **6**:71, *71*
radium **1**:19
radon **1**:25, 30
Rafflesia **5**:14
rail traffic control **10**:27
rail transportation **10**:20-27
railroads **1**:11; **8**:82; **9**:69, 74;
    10:20-27; **11**:80; **12**:75
    advantages of **10**:20
    cable-hauled **10**:26
    freight on **10**:27
    funicular **10**:28
    high-speed **10**:24-25; **12**:74, 75
    operation of **10**:27
    underground *see subways*
rain forest **3**:*76*, 77; **7**:8, 14-15, 18;
    12:52
    destruction of **7**:22-23; **12**:*50*
rain shadow desert **3**:84
rainbow **1**:*73*
rainfall **7**:21, 23; **12**:54
ram **8**:57
    hydraulic **8**:*57*
Ramapithecus **4**:27, *27*
rambutan **7**:*58*
ramie **7**:62
ramjet **12**:85
Rance River **9**:45
random access memory **11**:51
range finder **12**:13
    electronic **12**:13
rank **5**:62, 63, 83
rape, oilseed **7**:*61*
rats **7**:36, *36*
rattlesnakes **5**:50, 55

S

whooping cough **6**:66, 67; **12**:59
Wicken Fen, England **7**:*26*
widow bird (whydah) **5**:58
wild boar **5**:*57*
wild dogs **5**:49
wildebeest **5**:64, 78, *79*; **12**:55
wildlife **12**:52, 53
Wilkinson, John **8**:49
William Herschel reflector **12**:30
willow **3**:80
Wilson, Charles **1**:22
Wilson, Robert **2**:43
wind power **9**:42; **12**:57
wind turbine **9**:38, 42, 43, 48, 54
windmill **9**:54
windpipe **6**:18, *19*
winds **2**:67; **3**:70, *71*
   circulation **3**:*71*
   world pattern of **3**:*71*
wine production **8**:*52*
winged bean **7**:59
wings **4**:82
   in birds **5**:38
   in insects **5**:24
   see also airfoils
wireless **11**:31
withdrawal symptoms **6**:75
wolf spider **5**:27
wolves **5**:62, *66*, 70, *70*
womb *see uterus*
wood **8**:7, 8, 18
wood pulp **8**:8, 18, 19, 78, 79, *79*
woodchuck **5**:74
woodland **7**:9, 11, 27
woofers **11**:39
wool **7**:72; **8**:80
word processor **11**:9, 64, 68-69
World Health Organization *see*
   WHO
World Wildlife Fund (WWF) **7**:34,
   35
worm **5**:22
Wright brothers **10**:36, 39
wrybills **4**:39, *39*

X

X chromosome **6**:42
X-1 **9**:76
X-29 **12**:77
xenon **1**:30

X-ray diffraction spectroscopy
   12:37
X-ray tomography *see*
   computerized axial tomography
X-rays **1**:10, *76*; **2**:63; **11**:20, *20*, 31,
   74, 75; **12**:7, *31*, 38, 39, 60

Y

Y chromosome **6**:42
Yeager, Charles ("Chuck") **9**:76
yeast **5**:11
yeheb bush **7**:59
Yellowstone National Park **7**:27
Yerkes Observatory **12**:27
yew **5**:16
young (animals) **5**:64-65
Young, John **10**:64

Z

Zaire River **3**:77
Zambesi River **7**:*25*
Zambia **8**:11
zebra **3**:*79*; **7**:*29*
zebu cattle **7**:53, 54, 65, 68
Zelenchukskaya **12**:24
zeolites **1**:*37*
zeppelin **10**:36, 37
Zimbabwe **8**:14
zinc **1**:53; **8**:11
   smelting of **8**:32, *33*
zinc alloy **8**:55
zodiac **2**:12
zones **2**:63, 66
zooplankton **7**:*13*, *16*, 17
zygote **4**:59